The Obituary Of Richar╴ ... Being A Catalogue Of All Such Persons As He Knew In Their Life, 1627 To 1674

Richard Smith

THE

OBITUARY

OF

RICHARD SMYTH,

SECONDARY OF THE POULTRY COMPTER, LONDON:

BEING A CATALOGUE

OF

ALL SUCH PERSONS AS HE KNEW IN THEIR LIFE:

EXTENDING FROM A.D. 1627 TO A.D. 1674.

EDITED BY

SIR HENRY ELLIS, K.H.

PRINTED FOR THE CAMDEN SOCIETY.

M.DCCC.XL.IX.

PREFACE.

THE present volume has been printed from a transcript of the Sloane Manuscript in the British Museum No. 886, placed at the disposal of the Camden Society by Sir Charles George Young, Garter King of Arms.

The proof sheets have been collated with the Sloane MS.; this, however, is itself but a transcript, later than Smyth's time. Where the original manuscript of the Obituary is deposited is not at present known.

The best account of Richard Smyth is to be found in Wood's Athenæ Oxonienses, whose words we shall copy, subsequently making a few additions to the account of Smyth and his library; premising here, that in the parish register of Lillingston Dayrell, where he was born, and in his own signatures to the London Visitation in the Heralds' College, and to his Will, his name is uniformly spelt SMYTH; whilst upon his monument, and in the Register which records his burial at Cripplegate, it is spelt SMITH. Wood says,

"RICHARD SMITH, the son of a clergyman named Richard Smith, a native of Abingdon (by Martha his wife, daughter of Paul Darrel or Dayrell, of Lillingston Darrel, in Bucks, Esq.), son of Richard, son of another Richard Smith, of Abingdon, in Berks, sometime gent. usher to Qu. Elizabeth, was born at Lillingston Darrel before mentioned, an. 1590,* and after the beginning of the reign of James I. was sent to the university of Oxon., where, his stay being short, he was not matriculated, and therefore I cannot positively tell you of what College or Hall he was a member. Thence he was taken away by his parents, and put a clerk to an attorney belonging to the city of London; but, his mind hanging after learning, he spent all the time he could obtain from his employment in books. At riper years he became Secondary of the Poultry Compter† within the city of Lon-

---

* "Richard Smyth, the sonne of Richard Smyth, was baptized the 20. day of Sep', an'o D'ni 1590." Par. Reg. of Lillingston Dayrell.

† The following explanation of the history and functions of this office have been kindly supplied to the Editor by Mr. Serjeant Merewether, the present Town-Clerk of London.

"Sheriffs in Cities stand upon a different footing from those in Counties: London has the right to both: the right to elect two sheriffs for the city of London; and, the county of Middlesex having by one of the early charters been granted to the citizens, the two sheriffs of London are the sheriff of Middlesex. For the County, they exercise their functions, as in other counties, by an *Under-sheriff:* but in the City it is otherwise: each sheriff was responsible for his own officers; and therefore each sheriff had his own *Compter* or place where his officers accounted to the suitors for the debts they had received for them. These *Compters* were at last fixed in known places; one in the *Poultry,* and the other in *Wood Street.* Instead of one under-sheriff for both Sheriffs, each had his officer, who was called a SECONDARY, or the sheriff's second. Hence these two officers, who continue to the present day, and each performs the functions of an under-sheriff, and also certain contested elections, &c. &c. summoning jurors, &c.

"The Secondaries are usually lawyers, and hence Smith would be well acquainted in his day with those of his craft. It is a highly respectable station, of much responsibility and of some authority. The two present secondaries are Mr. James and Mr. Potter: both highly respectable men. Their station is probably nearly analogous to the station of masters and prothonotaries in the courts of law.

"In 1644, 20th Cha. I. October the 3d, Sir Richard Stone was discharged as Secondary for Wood Street Compter, and another to be admitted by the court of aldermen to try the right and title by a legal course: and on Oct. the 30th in the same year Mr. Nathaniel Hayes was discharged as Secondary of the Poultry Compter for insufficiency, and another to be admitted in the same manner. On Oct. 15th in the same year RICHARD SMITH was admitted as *Secondary of the Poultry Compter,* and John Reading for Wood Street. In 1655, eleven years after, Richard Smith surrendered up his place as Secondary of the Poultry Compter, and Edward Trotman was admitted in his place."

Edward Trotman's death is recorded in p. 88 of Smyth's Obituary.

don, a place of good reputation and profit, being in his time worth
about 700*l.* per an., which he executed many years; but upon the
death of his son, an. 1655 (begotten on the body of his wife Elizab.,
daughter of George Deane of Stepney), to whom he intended to
resign his place, he immediately sold it, and betook himself wholly to
a private life; two-thirds of which at least he spent in his library.
He was a person infinitely curious in, and inquisitive after books, and
suffered nothing considerable to escape him that fell within the compass of his learning, desiring to be master of no more than he knew
how to use. He was constantly known every day to walk his rounds
among the booksellers' shops (especially in Little Britain)* in London, and by his great skill and experience he made choice of such
books that were not obvious to every man's eye. He lived in times
which ministred peculiar opportunities of meeting with books that
were not every day brought into public light; and few eminent
libraries were bought where he had not the liberty to pick and chuse.
Hence arose, as that vast number of books, so the choiceness and
rarity of the greatest part of them, and that of all kinds and in all
sorts of learning, especially in history, of which he had the most considerable writers of all ages and nations, antient and modern, especially of our own and the neighbouring nations, of which, as 't was

---

* Little Britain, and Duck Lane in its immediate vicinity, were streets in which a large
number of the London booksellers in Smyth's time were congregated. Of those who inhabited the former street, the reader will find notices in pp. 9, 10, 21, 23, 27, 28, 38, 43,
50, 55, 61, 64, 66, 67, 69, 71, 74, 77, 79, 83, 86, 91, 93, 96, 97, 99, 102, and 103 ; of
those of the latter street, in pp. 17, 25, 34, 46, 54, 79, and 80. The entries of the deaths
of booksellers in every part of London are numerous.

Little Britain and Duck Lane were the Paternoster Row and Creed Lane of modern
times. Duck Lane is now Duke Street, Smithfield. The Ballards were the last of the old
race of booksellers who inhabited Little Britain.

thought, there was scarce any thing wanting that was extant. He
was also a great collector of MSS. whether antient or modern, that
were now extant, and delighted much to be poring on them. He collected also abundance of pamphlets published at and before the time of
reformation of religion, relating to ecclesiastical affairs, and it was sup-
posed that the copies of some of them were not then extant in the
world, and therefore esteemed as choice as MSS. Among the books
relating to history were his collection of lives, the elogia of illustrious
men, the authors who have written the lives and characters of writers,
and such who have writ of the foundations of monasteries. Nor was
he the owner of this choice treasure of books as an idle possessor, nor
did he barely turn over the leaves, but was a constant peruser of,
and upon his buying did generally collate them, observed the defects
of impressions, the ill arts used by many, and compared the differences
of editions; concerning which and the like cases he with great dili-
gence and industry entred many memorable and very useful remarks
and observations upon very many of his books under his own hand.
He hath written,

"*Letter to Dr. Hen. Hammond concerning the sense of that article
in the Creed,* 'HE DESCENDED INTO HELL.' Dated from his house
in Little Morefields, near London (where he mostly lived after he had
buried his son), in Apr. 1659; which letter being answered by Dr.
Hammond in the same month, were both afterwards published, an.
1684. See more in Dr. Hammond, under the year 1600. This
I think is all that R. Smith hath extant. Those things that are
not are these:

"*Treatise against Black Patches.* So Mr. Millington the bookseller.

"*Observations on the Three Grand Impostors.*

"*Exposition on these words used in the form of marriage,* 'WITH MY BODY I THEE WORSHIP.' Written in qu.

"*Collection of Expositions of Baptism for the Dead.* Wr. in qu.

"*Collection of several Expositions and Opinions of Christ's Descent into Hell.* See more in Dr. Hammond, before mentioned.

"*Miscellaneous Tracts, chiefly theological.*

"*Collection of arms belonging to the name of Smith, in colours.* MS. in oct.*

"*Vita S. Simonis Stock, Angli Carmelitæ.* Collected from the writings and MSS. of John Bale.

"*Life of Hugh Broughton, and Cat. of his works.*

"He also translated from Latin into English—

"1. *The Fifth Book of Histories of Corn. Tacitus.* 2. The *Order of receiving the new Bishop after his Consecration, before he enter into the Cathedral Church of Salisbury;* taken out of an old MS. ritual belonging to that church: and from French into English, *Bosquire's Sermon before the Company of Shoemakers in France, an.* 1614, on the festival of S. Crispin and Crispiana.

"Besides these and others of his writing and translations, he made ten thousand instances or remarks, with his own hand, of authors, either in or before the title or in the margin of their works.

"This Mr. Rich. Smith, who was a man of an excellent temper, great justice, &c. died 26 March, in sixteen hundred seventy and five, and was buried in the church of S. Giles's near to Cripplegate in London. Soon after was a marble monument erected over his grave for him, his wife, and children, with an inscription thereon,

---

* Such a collection, in 2 small vols. 8vo. is now in the Library of the College of Arms, but whether the same is not quite clear. They were in 1691 the property of George Ince, and afterwards in the Collection of John Warburton, Somerset Herald.

which for brevity's sake I shall now pass by. Afterwards there was a design to buy his choice library for a public use, by a collection of moneys to be raised among generous persons; but the work being public, and therefore but little forwarded, it came into the hands of Richard Chiswell, a bookseller living in S. Paul's churchyard, London; who printing a catalogue of, with others added to them, which came out after Mr. Smith's death, they were exposed to sale by way of Auction, and to the great reluctancy of public-spirited men, in May and June 1682."*

The monument of Smith, his wife, and sons, mentioned by Wood, is still to be seen against a pillar on the north side of the chancel of St. Giles's Cripplegate. Small figures of himself and his wife, in the attitude of prayer, on each side of a desk, appear in the upper part of the monument; and under the inscription recumbent figures of his two sons, still more diminutive in size. The following is the double Inscription:

"Mr. RICHARD
Smith, deceased y⁰ 26 of
March, 1675, aged 85."

"Neare this place lyeth interred Mrs. ELIZABETH SMITH, the wife of Mr. Richard Smith, sometymes Secondary of the Poultry Compter, by whom shee had 5 sonnes & 3 dauthters, whereof two onely suruiued her. Her life was pious & religious towards God, blamelesse towards men, exceeding pittiful and charitable to y⁰ poore and distressed, prudent & prouident in the ordering her family, haueing a great care & tender affection to her husband and to the instruˆon of her children & children's children in the fear of the Lord. Shee dyed the 25 of May, 1664, aged 64 yeares. Here also lyes buried 2 of her sonnes; John Smith, the eldest, beloued of all men for his affable deportment, admired for his more then ordinary guifts of nature. Hee dyed (to y⁰ great greife of his parents and frends) the 6ᵗʰ of May, 1655, aged 32 yeares; and Richard the youngest dyed in the 17ᵗʰᵉ yeare of his age, the 10ᵗʰ of August, 1653;

---

* Athenæ Oxon. edit. Bliss. vol. iii. col. 1031.

in comemoration of whom their tender & louing mother willed this monum' to bee erected, wch after her death was (by her appointment) at her owne priuate cost (by her frends) p'formed."

His will, dated 5th March 1669, was proved 12th April 1675, by Martha Hacker, his eldest daughter. It is written in a strain of piety, apparently by himself, and consists chiefly of money legacies to his near relations. His moveables, including his Books, he bequeathed to the favourite daughter and executrix who has been already mentioned as proving his will.

Beside the works of Smyth already mentioned, two others are preserved in manuscript in the Sloane Collection.

No. 338. "The Wonders of the World, collected out of divers approved Authors and learned Writers, by the industry of Richard Smith, Gent." 4to. and

No. 772. "Of the first Invention of the Art of Printing," 4to. upon a fly-leaf at the beginning of which is written, "This booke was written by my worthy good friend and diligent antiquary Richard Smyth, sometime Secondary of the Compter in the Poultry. Teste F. Barnard."

The Sale Catalogue of Smyth's library, with manuscript prices, formerly in Mr. Bindley's Collection, is now in the British Museum. Its Title, Address to the Reader, and Conditions of the Sale, will not be unacceptable; followed by a small selection of the prices brought by particular works. The catalogue is of the large quarto size, closely printed, and occupies no fewer than four hundred and four pages. The biddings in some instances appear to have advanced a penny at a time.

" Bibliotheca Smithiana ; sive Catalogus Librorum, in quavis Facultate In-
signiorum, quos in usum suum, et Bibliothecæ ornamentum, multo ære
sibi comparavit vir clarissimus doctissimusq. D. Richardus Smith Lon-
dinensis. Horum Auctio habebitur Londini, in Area vulgo dicta Great
St. Bartholomew's Close, in angulum ejusdem septentrionalem, Maij die
15, 1682.

" Per Richardum Chiswel, Bibliopolam.

" To The Reader.

" Though it be needless to recommend what to all intelligent persons will
sufficiently commend itself, yet perhaps it may not be unacceptable to the
ingenious to have some short account concerning this so much celebrated, so
often desired, so long expected, Library, now exposed to sale.

" The gentleman that collected it was a person infinitely curious and inquisitive after books, and who suffered nothing considerable to escape him that
fell within the compass of his learning ; for he had not the vanity of desiring
to be master of more than he knew how to use.   He lived to a very great
age, and spent a good part of it almost intirely in the search of books, being
as constantly known every day to walk his rounds through the shops as he
sat down to meals, where his great skill and experience enabled him to
make choice of what was not obvious to every vulgar eye.   He lived in
times which ministred peculiar opportunities of meeting with books that are
not every day brought into publick light ; and few eminent libraries were
bought where he had not the liberty to pick and choose.   And while others
were forming arms and new modelling kingdoms, his great ambition was to
become master of a good book.   Hence arose, as that vast number of his
books, so the choiceness and rarity of the greatest part of them, and that of
all kinds, and in all sorts of learning.

" No more need be instanced in than that of History, wherein here are the
most considerable historians of all ages and nations, ancient and modern,
and among them those especially of our own and the neighbour nations,
whereof I believe there is scarce any thing wanting that is extant ; and
among the Manuscripts several things that were never yet printed ; besides
abundance of Pamphlets publisht at and before the times of Reformation,
relating to ecclesiastical affairs, whereof it is reasonable to believe there are
no other copies now extant in the world (with multitudes of others of latter

times). Together with History may go along the Collection of Lives, "Elogia Virorum illustrium," the writers "de Scriptoribus," and of the Foundations of Monasteries, &c. perhaps the best and largest collection of that kind that is in any private library in this nation. Indeed the whole is so considerable that it is commonly known that the most learned men in these parts, and those who have the best libraries of their own, were wont frequently to have recourse to This, for things not to be had elsewhere.

" Nor was the owner of them a meer idle possessor of so great a treasure ; for, as he generally collated his books upon the buying of them (upon which account the buyer may rest pretty secure of their being perfect), so he did not barely turn over the leaves, but observed the defects of impressions, and the ill arts used by many; compared the differences of editions, concerning which and the like cases he has entred memorable and very useful remarks upon very many of the books, under his own hand; observations wherein certainly never man was more diligent and industrious.

" Thus much was thought fit to be communicated to publick notice by a gentleman who was intimately acquainted both with Mr. Smith and his books.

" This excellent library will be exposed by auction, and the sale will begin on Monday the 15th day of May next, at the auction house known by the name of the Swan, in Great St. Bartholomew Close, and there continued, day by day, the five first days of every week, till all the books be sold."

" The Conditions of the Sale are these:

" I. That he who bids most is the buyer ; and if any difference arise which the company cannot decide, then the book or books shall be forthwith exposed to sale again.

" II. That all the books in this catalogue, not otherwise expressed (for ought I know), are perfect ; but if any of them appear to be otherwise before they be taken away the buyer shall have his choice of taking or leaving them.

" III. That the money for the book or books so bought is to be paid by the buyer within one month after the auction is ended, at the place where they are sold, where constant attendance shall be given, for that month, day by day, from eight a clock to eleven, and from two till five, for receipt of the money and delivery of the books.

" IV. That the buyer and seller do mutually bind their respective executors and administrators to the performance of these conditions.

" V. That no person be admitted a buyer who, being a stranger to the seller or company, shall refuse to tell the place of his abode.

" VI. That no person be admitted a buyer that has refused or denied to pay for any books he has bought at any former auction.

> " For satisfaction of the buyers as to the condition of the books, they will be exposed to view at the place above mentioned, every day for a fortnight before the sale begins.
>
> " RICHARD CHISWELL."

" *March* 27. 1682.

The Missals, Horæ, and other Service books by our earliest printers, abounded in this library; as well as Tracts on Henry the Eighth's divorce; with a large Collection of the early Primers.

The prices at which some of the following articles sold will prove interesting to the bibliographer.

Pontificale Romanum (*cum Observationibus* R. SMITH *MSS. ex prioribus Edit.*) fol. Ven. 1543. £1.0.6.

Surius, Laur. de Vitis Sanctorum, ex probatis Authoribus et MSS. Codicibus (*cum Observat. MSS. per R. S. é Biblioth. Ecclesiast. Schultingii*), in 4 vol. fol. Col. Ag. 1617. £3.1.0.

Assertio Henrici VIII. Regis Angliæ Septem Sacramentorum adversus M. Luther. cum Orat. Jo. Clerk, et Bulla Pont. pro Confirmat. ejus Operis; item Epistola Regia admonitoria ad Duces Saxoniæ (*cum Observat. R. SMITH in varias edit. hujus Libri MSS.*) 4to Lond. 1521. £0.7.8.

Academiarum Italiæ et Galliæ Censuræ in Causa Matrimon. H. 8. cum relicta Fratris. 4to Lond. 1530. £0.16.0.

Buceri, M. Gratulatio ad Ecclesiam Anglicanam de Religionis Christi restitutione et de Colloquio Ratisbonæ & Cont. Steph. Gardiner. Episc. Wintoniensem. 4to 1548. £0.4.2.

Cochlei, Jo. Congratulatio disputatoria de Matrimonio Henrici VIII. Angliæ. 4to 1535. £0 3.4.

Manuale ad Usum Eboracensis Ecclesiæ. Lond. per Win. de Worde. 4to 1509. £0.8.2.

Martyrologium ad Usum Rom. cæterarumque Orb. Ecclesiarum per N. N. D. minorum (*cum Martyrologio S. Wilgefortis MS. per* R. SMITH), cui annex. MSS. in membraneis de gradibus xx. Virtutum à Sancto Ambrosio ordinatus, &c. 4ᵗᵒ Roth. 1507. £0.1.8.

Nicolai Papæ I. Epistola ad Mich. Imp. Ejusd. Decreta. Item Cochlæi Defensio Ioannis Ep. Roffen. & Th. Mori adversus R Samsonem. Item Frag. quarundarum T. Mori Epist. 4ᵗᵒ 1536. £0.2.0.

Henrici VIII. Regis Angliæ, &c. Orarium seu lib. Precationum Latinè. 8ᵛᵒ Lond. 1545. £0.1.4.

Testamentum Novum Latine, per Desid. Erasmum. 8° Bas. ap. Frobenium. 1523. £0.0.3.

Id. Latinè edita; et cum præfatione Martini Lutheri. 8° Bas. 1537. £0.0.3.

Monasticon Anglicanum per G. Dugdale, &c. in 3 vol. (fig.) fol. Lond. 1655-61-73. £5.1.0

Jo Capgravi Catalogus Sanctorum Angliæ. fol. Lond. per W. de Worde. 1516. £4.8.0.

M. Parker de Antiqu. Britannicæ Ecclesiæ, & Privilegiis Cantuar. &c. fol. Lond. 1572. £1.5.0. (A second copy sold for £2.1.0.)

Spelmanni Glossarium. opt. edit. (*cum Observat. MSS.* R. SMITH,) fol. 1664. £1.14.0.

Historia de Amore Edoardi 3. Regis Angliæ et Elipsiæ Comitissæ Salsbericencis. 8° 1612. £1.2.6.

A set of the Elzevirs which the French term " Les petites Republiques," in 48 volumes. £5.0.0.

Vita Reginaldi Poli Cardinalis & Cantuariensis Archiep. (*cum Testamento ultimo ejusd. MS. sub propria manu* R. SMITH.) 4ᵗᵒ Ven. 1563. £3.3.0.

Æsop's Fables, in very old English, and printed by Rich. Pynson (no title), fol. £0.1.2.

Bible, with M. Coverdale's Preface to K. Henry VIII (very fair). Fol. 1535. £1.0.6.

Books of Common Prayer, being the first of K. Edward the 6ᵗʰ. Lond. R. Graftoni, mense Martii 1549, fol. £1.15.0.

—— Another of K. Edward the VI. printed in the same year. Lond. Ed. Whitchurch, mense Junii. Fol. £1.5.0.

Books of Common Prayer. Another of K. Edward the VI. printed by
Ed. Whitchurch, fol. Lond. 1552. £1.1.0.

CAXTON, the first English printer, his Chronicle of England. Printed
1498. fol. £0.3.6.

———— Translation of the Knight of the Toure, out of French. fol. 1483.
£0 5.0.

———— Mirrour of the World, &c. (in very old English). Printed Anno
Dom. 1486. £0.5.0.

———— History of Jason touching the Conquest of the Golden Fleece (in
very old English). £0.5.1.

———— Recueile of the Histories of Troy, of the Destruction thereof,
&c. Lond. 1553. £0.3.0.

———— Ancient Treatise, intituled a Book of Good Manners, &c.
Lond. 1486. £0.2.0.

———— Translation of Cato, with many Hist. and Examples of Holy
Fathers, and Ancient Chronicles, &c. 1483, fol. £0.4.0.

———— Three Books more of the said Caxton (viz.) 1. Pilgrimage of
the Soul. 2. Chastising of God's Children. 3. The Rule of St. Benet
(all in very old English). £0 5.0.

———— Translation of Virgil's Æneides, in English prose. 1490. £0.3.0.

———— Game of Chess; it being, in Mr. Smith's opinion, one of the first
books which ever were printed in Engl. (*with Observations on the several
Editions of the same MS.*) 1474. £0.13.0.

———— Books entituled Vitas Patrum, or Lives of Old Ancient Fathers,
Hermites, &c. 1485. £0.8.0

———— Godfrey of Bulloigne, of the Seige and Conquest of Jerusalem
(*being K. Edward the* 4th's *own Book*). 1481. £0.18.0.

Dugdale's, W. Historical Account of the Baronage of England, two tomes
in one volume, fol. 1675. £1.8.0.

Froissart's Chronicles of England, France, Spain, Portugal, Scotland,
Britain, Flanders, &c. 1525. £0.10.0

Gerard's, John, Herbal, or General History of Plants, enlarged by Thomas Johnson, fol. 1636. £2.12.0.

Hollingshed's Chronicle of Engl. with the Addi. of many sheets that were
castrated (being not thought fit, and so not allowed to be printed in the second impression), in 2 vol. 1587. fol. £7.0.0.

History and Annals of Cornelius Tacitus by Sir Hen. Savile (with an Addi. of the 5th Book of the Hist. *translated by* R. SMITH *in MS.* it being omitted in Print), fol. 1612. £0.5.10.

Hackluyt's (R.) Navigations, Voyages, Trafficks, and Discoveries, &c. in 2 vols. 1599. £1.7.0.

Maunsell's, Andr. Catal. of Eng. printed B. (*with Addit. and Ob. of* R. SMITH, *MS.*) Lond. 1595. £0.3.6.

Polychronicon written by Ranulph Higden, Monk of Chester, fol. Lond. 1527. £1.0.2.

Rushworth's, Joh. Historical Collections in three vol. compleat (the first vol. *being of the first Edition not castrated, having the Pref. to* RICHARD CROMWELL). 1659-80.

Gospels of the Four Evangelists in Saxon and English, by Jn. Fox. 4° Lond. 1571. £0.13.0.

Bedwell's, W. Brief Descript. of Tottenham High Cross and Turnament of Tottenham, &c. 4° 1631. £0.2.6.

Fisher Bishop of Rochester. His Exposition on the Seven Penitential Psalms. 4to 1509. £0.1.0.

Harding's, John, Chronicle. 4° Lond. 1543. £0.8.0.

Holt, (Nic.) Master to Sir Thomas More his Acci. and Gram. (*with* R. S. *Acc. of the Au. MS.*) Ant. £0.0.2.

King Henry VIII. Institu. of a Christian Man, Exposit. of the Creed, X. Com. &c. 1537. £0.8.6.

——— Necessary Doctrine and Erudition for any Christian Man. 1547. £0.6.6.

——— Declaration of his just Wars with the Scots, and his just Right and Title to Scotl. 1542. 4to £0.2.4.

——— Answers to the Petitions of the Traitours & Rebels in Lincoln-shire and Yorkshire. 1536. 4to £0.2.2.

——— Articles for establishing Religion approv. by consent of the Clergy in Engl. 1536. 4to £0.0.6.

——— Goodly Primer in English, with Godly Meditat. and Pray. Printed upon Vellum. 1535. 4to £0.2.6.

——— Same again, printed upon Paper, at the same time. £0.1.6.

——— Primer in English and Latine, with a Preface by the said King Hen. the 8th. 4to 1545. £0.1.3.

King Henry VIII. Primer in English, with the Epistles and Gospels. Ibid. £0.1.3.

——— Epist. and Gosp. with a brief Postil upon the same by R. Tavern. Dedicat. to K. H. 8th. £0.1.6.

Psalter of David, translated into English by Rob. Crowley, time of Edw. 6th. (*with an Account of this Crowley by* R. SMITH *in MS.*) Lond. 1549. £0.0.4.

Psalter and Letany, with Hymns, time of Edw. the 6th. Lond. 1549. £0.0.6.

Expedition in Scotl. made by K. Henry the 8th Army under the conduct of the Earl of Hertf. 8º 1544. £0.1.7.

Uniform and Catholick Primer, Engl. Lat. with the Assent of Card. Pool. 4to Lond. 1555. £0 2.1.

The Mart. in Engl. after the Use of Sarum, and as it is read in Sion, with addit. by W. W. 4to 1526. £0.2.6.

Miracles of our Blessed Lady. Imprinted at Westminster in Caxton's House by W. de W. 4to £0.2.3.

Among bundles of stitched Books and Pamphlets we have—

Bundle of Proclamations, of Matters of State, principally in the Reigns of K. Henry 8th, Edw. 6th, K. Phil. and Q. Mary, Q. Eliz. One Proclamation of Q. Jane, 1553. Printed by Grafton. fol. £0.13.6.

Twelve merry Jests of the Lying widow Edyth, very old. A merry Play between the Pardoner and the Frere, very old Manner of consecrating Bishops, Priests, &c. Lond. 1559. A Pillar of Gratitude to the King and Parliament for restoring Episcopacy, 1661. John Ogilbye's Relation of the King's Entertainment through London, 1661. Bishop Usher's Mystery of the Incarnation of God, London, 1645. With seven more of Episcopacy, &c. £0.2.8.

Toward the end of the Catalogue—

" *Manuscripti, diversis Voluminibus.*"

Amongst these we have—

Form and Order of Consecration of Holy Virgins, partly in Latin and partly English, fairly written on Vellum, and bestowed on the Monastery of

Nunns of St. Mary in Westminster by R. Fox, Bishop of Winchester, in folio. £0.13.10.

J. Capgravius (à monumento pileato sic suo sensu nominat.) de diversis symbolis Fidei (ab ipso congestis) Opus edidit, idemque D. Willielmo Gray Eliensis Episc. sub Hen. 6. 1454, dedicavit : et pulchrè in membraneis conscriptus. Fol. £0.3.4.

Escurialis Monasterii S. Laurentii Orbis Miraculi Descriptio, partim Latinè partim Anglicè *ex variis authoribus collecta per* R. SMITH. Folio. £0.2.8.

Lib. de Priorat. de Belvoir, 2. Martyrologium Romanum, 3. Calendarium. 4. Ordinationes seu Statuta Benedicti XII. P. Ord. nigrorum Monach. 5. Ordinationes Thomæ Abbatis S. Albani A. D. 1360, cum aliis de Prioratu et Conventu de Belvoir (in membranis). Fol. £0.15.6.

Description of the City of Winchester, with an historical Relation of divers memorable Occurrences touching the same, with a Preamble of the Origin of Cities in general, by J. Trussell. Folio. 12s.

The whole Parliament Roll, containing the Acts of King Richard the Third, the manner how he took on him the Crown, and other considerable passages about the same. Fol. £5.1.0.

Six several Catalogues of all such Books, touching as well the state Ecclesiastical as Temporal of the Realm of England, which were published upon several occasions, in the Reigns of King Henry the Seventh and Henry the Eighth, Philip and Mary, Q. Elizabeth, K. James, and Charles I. *Collected by Mr. H. Dyson; out of whose library was gathered, by Mr.* SMITH, *a great part of the rarities of this Catalogue.* £0.7.6.

A great Bundle of Sermons, &c. of Mr. Richard Smith of Stilton (father of R. S. late proprietor of this library) written with his own hand, and by him preached partly at Brasted in Kent and partly at Stilton aforesaid ; with a Catalogue of every particular Serm. &c. contained in the Bundle by R. Smith, son to the aforesaid R. Smith. £0.15.0.

A small Manuscript of Mr. Richard Smith's Observations concerning the Three Grand Impostors. 4to £0.3.0.*

His Collection of several Expositions and Opinions of Christ's Descent into Hell, with his Conference with Mr. Selden about that Argument; and

---

* Now, MS. Sloane, Brit. Mus. No. 1024.

a Letter to Dr. Hammond, touching the sense of that Article conceived by Mr. Selden, and Dr. Hammond's Answer thereunto. Quarto. £0.10.0.

His Translation of Bosquier's Sermon before the Company of Shoemakers in France, 1614, On the Festival of St. Crispin and Crispiana. 4to £0.2.6.

His Exposition on these Words used in the Form of Marriage, "With my Body I thee worship." 4°. £0 1.3.

His Collection of Expositions of Baptism for the Dead. 4to £0.2.6.

A Bundle of Miscellaneous Tracts (chiefly Theological), with some Translations by Mr. Smith and others, written with his own hand. 4to £0 1.2.

Something must now be said of the OBITUARY itself.

A few Extracts from it are preserved in the Harleian MS. 3361, in the handwriting of John Bagford: and a Selection, perhaps to the amount of a fourth part, was made from its entries, and printed by Peck, in the second Volume of the "Desiderata Curiosa." But even he did not see the points in which its best value consists.

For the period through which it extends, it is a useful Record for the Citizens of London; and for any one engaged in a work intended to illustrate the History of the Metropolis during Smyth's time, almost indispensable.

Dugdale, in his "Origines Juridiciales," gives no List of the Heads of the Law in this country from 1640 to 1660; nor is the deficiency, the Editor believes, supplied in any other printed work. Smyth was a member of the profession; and, as far as a Law-Necrology goes, has filled the hiatus.

In the Catalogue of Sir William Musgrave's Prints, in the Tenth Day's Sale, No. 82, we find a contemporary Portrait of " Richard Smith; virtuoso and literary character," engraved by " W. Sherwin." This was our Richard Smyth. The purchaser of it was Sir Mark Masterman Sykes, at the price of £7. 17. 0. At Sir Mark Sykes's

sale it was again sold for £5. 5. 0.: and is believed to have been
bought for Richard Heber, Esq.: but the editor of the present
volume has been unable to trace it further, or to obtain the know-
ledge of any other Impression. Bromley, in his " Catalogue of
Engraved British Portraits," p. 129, says, " I never saw this Print."

It has been already shown that Smyth was a man of good family,
well connected; as is further seen in the accompanying Pedigree,
which has been obligingly communicated by Sir Charles Young from
the Records of the College of Arms. It illustrates many of the entries in the Obituary. Smyth however, throughout the placid tenor
of his life, never failed to chronicle in it the deaths of his relations and
connexions, however humble their condition in society might have
become.

PEDIGREE OF RICHARD SMYTH,

FROM THE RECORDS OF THE COLLEGE OF ARMS.

Ph. 1, p. 10 ; C. 24, 3b ; K. 9, 226.

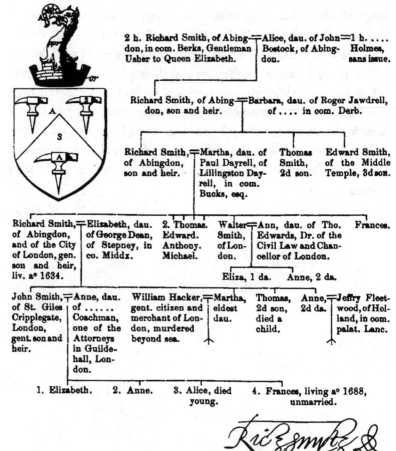

2 h. Richard Smith, of Abing-⊤Alice, dau. of John⊤1 h. ....
don, in com. Berks, Gentleman | Bostock, of Abing- | Holmes,
Usher to Queen Elizabeth. | don. | sans issue.

Richard Smith, of Abing-⊤Barbara, dau. of Roger Jawdrell,
don, son and heir. | of .... in com. Derb.

Richard Smith,⊤Martha, dau. of | Thomas | Edward Smith,
of Abingdon, | Paul Dayrell, of | Smith, | of the Middle
son and heir. | Lillingston Day- | 2d son. | Temple, 3d son.
| rell, in com. |
| Bucks, esq. |

Richard Smith,⊤Elizabeth, dau. | 2. Thomas. | Walter⊤Ann, dau. of Tho. | Frances.
of Abingdon, | of George Dean, | Edward. | Smith, | Edwards, Dr. of the
and of the City | of Stepney, in | Anthony. | of Lon- | Civil Law and Chan-
of London, gen. | co. Middx. | Michael. | don. | cellor of London.
son and heir, |
liv. aº 1634. | | | Eliza, 1 da. | Anne, 2 da.

John Smith,⊤Anne, dau. | William Hacker,⊤Martha, | Thomas | Anne,⊤Jeffry Fleet-
of St. Giles | of ...... | gent. citizen and | eldest | 2d son, | 2d da. | wood, of Hol-
Cripplegate, | Coachman, | merchant of Lon- | dau. | died a | | land, in com.
London, | one of the | don, murdered | | child. | | palat. Lanc.
gent. son and | Attorneys | beyond sea. | | |
heir. | in Guilde- |
| hall, Lon- |
| don. |

1. Elizabeth.   2. Anne.   3. Alice, died   4. Frances, living aº 1688,
                              young.   unmarried.

The fac-simile of Smyth's autograph, here given, is from the entry in the Visitation of
London, 1634 ; the latter part of the Pedigree being from the later Visitation of 1688.

OBITUARY

OF

RICHARD SMYTH.

A CATALOGUE

OF

ALL SUCH PERSONS DECEASED

WHOME I KNEW IN THEIR LIFE TIME,

WHEREIN ARE SET DOWN

THE SEVERAL YEARS OF OUR LORD, AND THE DAYES OF THE MONTH

WHEN

EVERY ONE OF THEM DYED OR WERE BURIED,

FROM THE

YEAR OF OUR LORD M.DC.XXVIII. SUCCESSIVELY.

SMITH'S OBITUARY.

1606.

October   8. My grandfather, Paul Dayrell, Esqr. buried at Lillingston Dayrell.

1627.

March   12. Dr. Lamb killed in the Old Jurie by a rude multitud, for which the City was fined.

19. The Earle of Devonshire dyed.

21. My uncle Walter Dayrell dyed at Graies Inne.

23. My cozen Brigit Dayrell, eldest daughter of my uncle Francis Dayrell, dyed at Edmonton.

1628.

August 11th. My son Richard, the first of that name (a twinn), dyed between 7 and 8 in the morning, and buried at St. Michael's church in Cornhill, wher he was nursed.

23. George Duke of Buckingham, stabed to death at Portsmouth in Capt. Mason's house by one John Felton.

Septemb. 1. Foulk Grevil, Lord Brooke, stabed to death with a knife by his servant Ralph Hayward, who with the same knife stabed himselfe also, whereof he also instantly died.

Octob. 24. Geo. Mountain, A.Bp. of York, late Bp. of London, died.

25. Anth. Culverwell, attorn. in Wood Street, died.

Novemb^r. 2. Sir John Osborn, of the Exchequer, died.

23. Mrs. Steed, in the Old Jurie, died.

29. Jo. Felton, that killed the D. of Buckingham, executed at Tyborn.

29. Mr. Thomas Wood (comonly called Velvet Wood) died.

Decembr. 14. My uncle Euseby Andrews died.

21. Mis Gale, in ye Old Jewry, leaping out of a garret-window into her neighbour's yard, broke her neck.

25. Alderman Allen Cotton, Kt. died of a gangreen.

January 14. News brought of the Palsegraves eldest sonn drowned in Harlem Meer, in Holland.

17. Edward Sugar, apothecary, died.

March 14. Sir James Leigh, Lord Treasurer, Earle of Marlborough, died, an old man, and of good report.

15. Mis Lucas, wife to Anthony Lucas, upholsterer, died.

1629.

March 26. Henry Awdley, an attorn. of the Common Pleas, died of a wound given him by thieves at Ilford.

April 4. Edward Whiterduce, baker in Coleman Street, buried.

5. John Cox, in Cony Hoop Lane in ye Poultry, died.

May 9. Alderman Hodges, in Walbrook, this night died.

13. This night Q. Mary miscarried of her first male child, dying imediatly after it was born, yet baptized.

July 10. Sergant Major Dawson and 4 or 5 others dyed for a tumult by the Templers, raised about an arrest.

16. James Wood, chandler in Distaff Lane, died.

Mis Hough, wife of Ralph Hough in Lothbury, died.

John Stamford &} gentl. {hanged at Tyborn, condemned
Nich. Ashenhurst} {of a murther in Fleet Street.

28. Paul Lord Banning died.

Novemb^r. 13. Mr. Leeche's wife (minister at Bow Church), drowned herself in the Thames; taken up at Cuckold's Point.

January 18. Griffin Robinson, an attorn. died.
    24. Sir Henry Yelverton, one of the judges of the Common Pleas, died.

Februar. 22. Old Farnaby, parish clerk in the Old Jury, buried.

1630.

March 28. Richard Camill, of the Petty Bagg, died.

Apr.   9. Radford, our Exigent Retorner, buried.
    10. Wm. Earl of Pembrok died of an apoplexie at Baynard's Castle.

May 10. Mr. Robert Blackwell, of the Petty Bag, buried.

May   Mr. Bill, the King's printer, buried.
    Mr. Brereton, a mercer, buried.
    Woodcook, a vintner at the corner of Silver Street in Great Wood Street, burnt in his bed.
    Wm. Earl of Northampton died.
    Sim. Franter, Clerk of the Exchequer, buried.
    Mr. Tho. Bateman, of Osborn's office in the Exchequer, buried.

Aug. 16. Mr. Sheerrat, the baker, buried.
    23. Mr. Andrew Milmaster, of the Old Jury, died.

Octob.   Oliver Severmeer, sometime my father's servant, died at St. Katherine by the Tower.

Nov.   5. Rebecca Burt, once servant at Mr. Hutchinson's in Poultry, our old acquaintance, dyed.
    18. Sir John Walter, Lord Chief Baron, died.
    24. Nath. Maureick, chief clerk to the Town Clerck, died.

Decemb. 3. Mr. Thom. Steed, grocer, our comon-councelman, in the Old Jury, died.

Febr. 26. Edward Evans, once Mr. Ednoy's clerk, died of the plague, no other but himself that week in London dying of the plague.
    March, Apr. 1630-1, and May 1631, there dying none.

1631.

May   Sir Robert Cotton, the famous antiquary, died.

14. Tuchet, Lord Audley, condemned for . . .
and was beheaded on Tower Hill.

21. Clerk of the Errors of the Comon Pleas died.

June   1. Mr. Martyn, a rich citizen in Milk Street, died.

2. Richarn Crashaw, a rich citizen of the Exchange, died.

3. Sim. Yong, haberdasher, in Fleet Street, died of a sur-
fett.

4. Henry Fryer, Esqr. in Little Britain, by a fall from
his horse bruised, died.

id. Thomas Newton, Clerk of the Excheq. died. .

10. Captn. Nich. Leat died.

Aug.   12. Sir Thomas Middleton, alderman, died.

Decem.   5. Captn. Benjam. Henshaw died.

6. Wm. Deane, my wives brother, died.

7. Sir Hugh Middleton (brother to Sir Thomas Middleton) died.

12. Sir Thomas Fanshaw, Kt. died.

28. Mr. Wm. Langhorn, attorn. King's Bench, died.

1631-2.

Jan.   21. Thom. Leech, a scrivener, clerk-sitter in Wood Street
Compter, died.

1632.

March   26. Sir Thom. Lemon, alderman, died.

Apr.   1. Dr. Butts, Vice Chancellr of Cambridge, hanged himself, being Easter Day.

2. Mr. Davis, Sir Rand. Crew's clerk, drowned in the
River Lee, was this day buried in Barking Church.

16. Mr. Creak, a preacher, hanged himself in his garter, at
Mr. Turner's in Watling Street.

20. Mr. Bland, a merchant in St. Syth's Lane, died suddenly.

A woman burnt in Smithfield for poisoning her husband.

June   2. Robt. Cromwell, servant to Joseph Lane, attorn. in
Fetter Lane, hanged for poysoning his master.

July   15. Tilney Couchman, attorn. of Guildhall, died.

         15. My aunt Smith, wife to my uncle Thomas Smith, died
at Thorn in Yorkshire.

August   Justice Whitlock⎫
                &   ⎬died both this vacation.
            Justice Harvey ⎭

         24. Rich. Collyns, a yoeman of Wood Street Compter, died.

         28. Rich. Bretton, attorn. of the King's Bench, of Davies *
Inne, died.

Sept.   4. Mᶦˢ Lewis, in Old Jewry, died.

          5. John, Mr. Barker's man, buried.

Octob.   24. My uncle Sutton died.

Novem.   The Earle of Northumberland died.

          6. The King of Sweden slayne in battell.
            The Palsgrave K. of Bohemia died this month.

          9. My little son Willm. (a twyn) died.

Feb.   12. Geo. Perkins, attorn. died, next day after the great fire
on London Bridge.

         12. Mr. Meredith, a rich citizen of Smithfield, walking in
the feilds, sudenly died.

         14. Mr. Edm. White, a rich citizen in St. Lawrence Lane,
was burᵈ.

         15. Toby Johnson, dier in Thames Street, our familiar ac-
quaintance, buried.

Mar.   15. Wm. Gittins, a surgeon in Coleman Street, some time
servant to old Mr. Cha. Friderick, cutt his own throat.

1633.

May   1. Mr. Lewes Marbury, attorn. died.

---

* Thavies Inn.—ED.

Mis Hatt died.

July   18. Mis Bromfield (our neigbor) buried at Stepny.

Oct^r.   4. Geo. Abbot, A.Bp. of Canterbury, died.

Sept.   9. Robt. Shuckforth, grocer, churchwarden, died.

Octob.   1. Harford, a barber in Smithfield, poysoned himself.

      6. Tho. Baker, attorn. Guildhall, died.

    22. Saml. Wilson, vintner, at the Nag's Head in the Old Jury, died.

    28. Mis Newbold, Old Jewry, died in child bed.

Nov^{br}.   14. Mr. Newbold's young child died.

    27. Arth. Groghagan, an Irish Dominican Frier, executed at Tiborn for traytorous words spoken in Spain, that he would kill the King, which at his death he denyed.

    28. John Davis, scrivener in Coleman Street, died.

Decem.   5. Mr. Fyncher, Mr. Green's clerk in the Old Jury, died.

    6. Four felons sent to the warres, after they were condemned returned again, were convict of other felonies, and hanged at the 4 gates, Aldersgate, Criplegate, Bishopsgate, and Algate.

    11. Mis Garland, in Coleman Street, died.

    11. Captⁿ John Haulsey, fishmonger, died.

    12. A taylor's wife, for killing her husband, burnt in Smithfield.

Jan.   5. Mis Herbert, in Wood Street, died.

    8. Mich. Plomb, attorn. in Wood Street, died.

    12. Otho Gayer died.

    15. Sir Edw. Barkham, alderman, died.

    17. Tho. Dyson, son of Hum. Dyson, Old Jury, died.

    18. Harman Sheppard, hanged in Smithfield; . . women and one man at Tyborn.

    21. Robert Robinson, a cutler, hanged in Smithfield for ravishing (his) wives daughters.

    21. One Ward hanged in Grays Inne Lane for killing one Thomas there.

Feb. · 12. Mr. Fenton, the chirurgeon, died.

17. Mr. Thurlby, attorn. of Oundle, died.

19. Mr. Staple, attorn. in Barbican, buried.

22. Vincent Bayord, one of Mr. Mathew Burked's clerks, hanged in Guildhall yard for stabbing one of his fellow clerks with his knife.

22. Mis Wase, wife to Mr. Wase bookseller in Little Britain, died.

23. Mis Saunders, wife to Mr. Hugh Saunders of Clifford's Inn, died.

Mar. 10. A seaman hanged at Browns Well beyond Highgate for killing a tincker there.

16. Sir Ralph Freeman, alderman, died.

21. Mr. Duncomb, attorn. Comon Pleas and Exchequer, died.

1634.

Apr. 29. Tho. Sayer, messenger of the Court of Wards, died.

May 15. Rich. Lawley, innkeeper at the George without Aldersgate, buried.

June 12. Sir Robt. Ducy, Kt. and Bart. alderman, Lond. died.

July 2. Sir Mart. Lumley, Kt. alderman, London, died.

9. Gawin Wetson, attorn. Exchequer, buried.

10. Anthony Sturdivant, comfit maker, buried.

10. Tho. Turpyn, serjeant at mace, a fencer, died.

Augt. 9. Wm. Noy, Esqr. ye King attorn. died at Brainford.

Mr. Emor Bickley, brother to my coz. Thomas Bickley, late secondary, died.

Sept. 3. Sir Edw. Coke, late Lord Chief Justice, first of the Comon Pleas, then of the King's Bench, died.

7. Sir Thomas Hamond, Knt. died at Hardres in Kent.

13. Old Mr. Lloyd, secondary of Wood Street Compter, died.

Dec. 9. Old Thomas Norman, serjeant at mace of Wood Street Compter, died.

15. Hen. Hutchinson, of the Poultry, died in Virginia.
22. Old Mr. Ricroft, in the Old Jury, died.
   Sir Wm. Paddy, doctor of physick, died.
   The Countess of Leicester died.
   Rich. Barnet, attorney King's Bench, buried.

Jan. 28. Mr. Mich. Low, secondary of Wood Street, died.
28. Mis Rawlinson, of the Old Jury, died.

Feb. 4. Sir Thom. Richardson, Lord Chief Justice of the King's
   Bench, died; his monument is in Westminster
   Abbey, against the cloysters.
   Old Walter Spencer, a recusant, died.
11. Rich. Winter, attorn. of the Comon Pleas, died of a
   consumption.
11. Stephen Bunce, attorn. of the King's Bench, died.
18. Deputy James Trott, in Cheapside, died.
18. ——— Chester, attorn. of the King's Bench, who married Mr. Garland's daughter of Coleman Street, died.
22. Rich. Wase, bookseller in Little Britaine, died.

Mar. 8. Geo. Crooket, our bag-bearer, died.
12. Rich. Lord Weston, Lord Treasurer, died.
15. Sir Robt. Cock, Clerk of the Check, died.
16. Sim. Waterson, bookseller, died.
   Mr. Bincks, cook in ye Old Jury, died.
   Mr. Dobbins, attorn. at Lyon's Inne,
   Mr. Rosogan, attorn. at Lyon Inne,
   Sergeant Ryng,   } Died all this
   Mr. Wood, toll-taker in Coleman St^t, Vacation.
   Thom. Howard, Earle of Suffolke,

1635.

Apr. 14. Tho. Sherwood hanged in chains in Grays Inne Fields
   for the murther of Mr. Claxton and Holt.
17. Elizb. Evans hanged also there for ye same murther.

Wm. Haylock, fishmonger, died this month.

May 8. John Blyth, attorn. of Clifford's Inne, my familiar friend, died.

8. Sir Horatio Vere's funerall, who died of an appoplex.

Fran. Dorrington, attorn. about this time died.

June 4. Old Geo. Newton, the yeoman, buried.

6. Robt. Wright, sergeant at mace, Wood Street, died.

7. James Blanchor (of the Bridg) died suddenly.

21. John Croome, attorn. once Mr. Cappedick's clerk, of the King's Bench court, hanged himself.

27. John Smith, of the Exigents Office in the Comon Pleas, died of a squimcie.

July 21. Geo. Cotton, of the Old Jury, upholster, died.

Alderman Deane about this time died.

August About this time Mis Price, my wives midwife, died.

Mr. Wm. Darby and Mr. Bradshawe } attornies of ye King's Bench, both died this Vacation.

9. Sim. Thorogood, linen draper, died.

13. Mis Vaughan, our neighbour in the Old Jury, buried.

30. Nich. Smith, keeper of the Poultry Compt^r^, died.

Oct. 30. Mr. Lewes Bromhall, attorn. died.

Novr. 14. Old Wm. Parr, aged 152 years, died.

Decem. 9. Tho. Turnor, clerk-sitter, Poultry Compt^r^, died.

10. Mis Holland at the Black Raven in Cheapside, wife to Hen. Holland, stationer, died of a wolfe.

12. Wm. North hanged against the Compter in Wood Street for stabbing his owne wife to death.

20. Mr. Mason, Recorder of London, died; once secondary of the Poultry Compter.

23. My cozen, Thomas Bitcliff ye elder, died.

25. Sir Randall Cranfield, of Coleman Street, died.

26. Sir Walter Pye, attorney of the Court of Wards, died.

26. Mis Claver, of Oning, about this time died.

Mr. Francklyn, attorn. of the King's Bench, died.

Feb.   16. Fran. Chapman, goldsmith in Lombard Street, died of a fall downe the staires.

Jan.   2. Mr. Rich. More, of the Old Jury, died.

     8. Mr. Robt. Browler, cloathworker in Lothbury, died.

Mar.   3. Geo. Chamberlyn, vintner at the Miter in Wood Street, died of a consumption; buried ye 8. day.

     11. Edw. Erby, solicitor, clerk of the plaisterers, hath died in his bed sodainly.

     13. Ben. Paul, vintner at ye St. John's Head, died.

     17. Mr. Townson, fishmonger in Old Fish Street, died.

1636.

March   30. Thom. Mustard, merchant, died.

Apr.   8. Mr. Tho. Josselyn, of the Exchequer, buried.

     Mr. Bancroft, of the Exchequer, about ye same time.

     17. Sir Julius Cæsar, M^r of the Rolls, died.

     25. Sir James Haies, Earle of Carlisle, died; his funerall May 6.

May   4. Geo. Lindsey, messenger of the Poultry Compter, died.

     6. Alderman Wright's wife died.

     9. Mis Crook, Mr. Moses Tryon's daughter, died.

     17. Mr. Trussell, in Warwick Lane, died.

     18. Mr. Barton, a taylor at Puddle Wharf, died.

     22. Mr. Phillips, a vintner at ye Flying Horse in Wood Street, died.

     27. Sir Wm. Curteene, Kt. died.

May   31. Edw. James, Clerk of Newgate, died.

June   4. Susan Day, of the Old Jury, died.

     6. Old Mis Frederick, of the Old Jury, buried.

     9. Owen Arthur, mercer, of Cheapside, died.

     11. Humfrey Powell, exigent clerk in Wood Street, died.

July   Mr. Pipe, late secondary of the Poultry Compter, died about this time, whome Mr. Haies succeeded.

Feb.   21. Mr. Mottershead, of the High Comission, died.

     25. Mr. Newman, of the Starr Chamber, died.

27. Tho. Freeborn, in the Old Jury, died.

Mar. 1. Tho. Masters, goldsmith of Milk Street, died.

20. Sir Wm. Code, of King's Langley, died in Aldersgate Street.

20. Mr. Barton, a vintner in Gracechurch Street, cutt his owne throat.

1637.

Mar. 31. Wm. Tiffin, mercer, died of ye plague.

May 17. Valentin Bolles, vintner, died.

17. Stephen Chappell, vintner, died.

17. Edw. Alsop (called Deputy Tagg) died.

17. More Fortune, bayliff of St. Martin's, died.

Aug. 9. My cozen Paul Colton died.

19. Mr. Slye the baker died.

20. Sir Henry Calthrop, Recorder, died.

Sept. My aunt Mary Sutton about this time died.

My cozen Megg Bitcliff about this time died.

2. Mr. Hugh Sanders, attorn. buried.

5. Mr. Rich. Glover, of Great St. Bartholomew's, once depending on my Lord Ch. Justice Hubard, died.

Tho. Darbyshire, attorn. died about this time.

14. Capt. John Willams, goldsmith in Cheapside, died.

27. Edw. Lord Denny, Earle of Norwich, died.

Mr. Frith, preacher at St. Alphage, died.

Novr. 27. Mr. Hemington buried at Lauley.

Countess of Northumberland died of the small pox.

Dec. 15. Mie Dawes, at ye Dagger in Friday Street, died.

23. My uncle Edward Smith died.

Jan. 13. Thom. Jervis, turnkey of the Compter in Wood Street. died.

14. Mr. Howkens, at Grocers' Hall, died.

Mr. Cole, Mr. Augustin Garland's son-in-law, died.

Mr. Covile, of Sir Miles Fleetwood's office, died.

Mr. Lewin, of the Water works, died.

22. Old Mr. Augustin Garland, attorn. in Coleman Street, died.

Feb. 6. Rich. Alport, son of Richard Alport, upholsterer in the Poultry, buried.

7. John Edwards, brother to my brother Walter Smith's wife, buried.

21. Mr. Sounds, chief usher of Paul's School, died.

Sir Hen. Wotton, Kt. Provost of Eaton Colledge, about this time died.

25. Dr. Francis White, Bp. of Ely, died.

27. Mr. Child, scrivenor, died sodenly.

29. Old John Broughton, of Stilton, died.

Mar. 7. Mr. Joshua Gallard, of St. Lawrence Lane, died.

Mr. Dr Watson, of Aldermary parish, sometime vicar of St. Stephen's Coleman Street, died about this time.

1638.

April 22. Nathaniell Mitchell (a monyed man) died.

24. Old Mr. Char. Eland buried.

May 6. Nich. Hart, attorn. died.

June 1. Nath. Sampson, late Under-Sheriff of Middlesex, died.

July 6. Mis Worthington, in Fetter Lane, died.

9. Mr. Hamlet, clerk of the Lord Mayor's Court, died.

21. Lawr. Hill, grocer in Wood Street, died.

21. Christoph. Coleman, oyleman there, died.

21. Mis Smith of Norbury, wife of Parson Mich. Smith, died.

25. Clement, Mr. Henry Aire's maid in Wood Street, died.

22. Mr. Rich. Brownlow, prothonotory, died.

31. Mis Tench, of Langley, died.

August.   Robt. Downes, attorn. of Furnivall's Inne, died about this time.

8. Hen. Needler, cruellman, died.

11. Mr. Nathan Shute, preacher in the Poultry, died.

August 13. Alderman Geo. Andrews died in Walbrook.

16. Sir John Bowyer buried.

28. My good old father, Mr. Rich. Smith, died at Stilton. Baptiz. ye 3d. of Novemb. 1567; died aged 71.

Mr. Robt. Moyle, prothonotory,

Mr. Alderman Hum. Smith,

Mr. Wm. Hodges, in Paternoster Row, } all died about the end of this month.

Gregory Oldfield, Comon Hunt,

Dr. Patrick Sanders, of St. Helen's,

Septemb. 1. Geo. Besse, attorn. in ye Poultry, died.

3. Middleton, book-keeper, Poultry Compter, died.

10. Rabbi Lanc, silkman, buried.

19. Mr. Hugh Dashfield, my Lord Coventry's gentleman, buried.

October 5. Mis Popham, of ye Old Jury, died.

22. James Cabell, in Milk Street, died.

Novem. 9. Dan. Eyres, keeper of Wood Street Compter, died. Wm. Wilson, solicitor in ye Exchequer, died.

10. Alderman Robt. Cambell died.

19. Finch, a cuttler and sollicitor, found dead in Perpool Lane, with his neck broke.

20. Edw. Cresner, clerk of the papers in Wood Street Compter, died.

December 6. Alderman Tho. Moulson died; buried 10th January.

6. Mr. Robinson, six clerk, died.

Jan. 6. Old Mis Harey, our neighbour in Old Jury, died; buried ye 10. of January.

6. Baron Denham died.

25. Judge Hutton died.

26. Old Johnson, bricklayer in Wood Street, died.

March 13. Tho. Newton, chandler in Coleman Street, died.

18. Sir Dudly Diggs, M^r of the Rolls, died.

1639.

April 10. Math. Isham, of Edmonton, died about this time.

14. Tho. Houff, Bucklers Bury, (that sold the nappy Ale,) died.

22. Edw. Thornton, attorn. died.

May 4. Dr. Stoughton, of Aldermanbury, died.

8. Mis Bowyer, Old Jury, died.

June 4. John Phillips, serjeant, Wood Street Compter, died.

July 28. Christoph. Grey, vintner, died.

Aug. 18. Sir Rich. Fen, alderman, died.

Septr. 20. Sir Thom. Edmonds died.

Mr. Eaton, surgeon,
Mr. Napkyn, surgeon,
Mr. Tho. Cotton, attorn. Excheq.
Mr. Rogers, clerk of the Cloth workers,
Mr. Smith, tobbaconist at Aldersgate,

    all dyed this month of September.

Octob^r. 7. The Dutchess of Richmond buried.

Decemb. 16. Justice Vernon died about this time.

Jan. 14. Thom. Lord Coventry, Lord Keeper, died about this time.

28. Rich. Furner, of Great Baddow, gentl. died.

1. Tho. Carter, ironmonger in ye Poultry, died.

6. Rogers, a goldsmith, died in Newgate.

12. Young Mis Waterhouse, in Cheapside, died.

13. Deputy Wm. Tully, in St. Martin's, died.

Feb. 7. Robt. Hall, attorn. Comon Pleas, about this time died.

10. Robt. Erdswell, of the Prerogative Court, died.

29. Geo. Brittan, attorn. Comon Pleas, and clerk of Skinners' Hall, died.

March 13. Mr. Topp, who married Mis Elizabeth, daughter of Sir Tho. Hamond, died. He gave a legacie to my brother Walter.

1640.

May 29. Old Mr. Grice, in Aldersgate Street, who wore trunck breeches, died.

———— Howard, Earle of Suffolk, Lord Warden of the Cinque Ports, died.

Old Lady Camble, in Coleman Street, about this time died.

Mr. Nealand, bookseller in Duck Lane, died.

12. Mis Almery, first wife of Mr. Geo. Almery, died.

Mr. Knightbridg, attorn. in Chelmsford, died.

Old Tho. Stock, of Sewardston in Essex, died.

31. Old Mr. Hanson, of Whittington Colledge, died.

27. Hen. Little, haberdasher within Ludgate, near Paul's, died.

June   10. Sir Maur. Abbot, alderman, died.

15. Alderman Sam. Gilnmer died.

July   1. Helmdon, crier in the Exchequer, died.

3. Edw. Roberts, a clerk in the Compter, died.

12. Ben. Portlock, Senr, attorn. died.

26. Alderman Rudge died.

Mr. Guy, an attorn. killed with the kicking of a stone horse.

Aug^t.   6. Mr. John Stone, in Coleman Street, sergeant at law, died.

7. Mr. Geo. Humble, in Pope's Head Alley, died.

8. My son Thomas died.

14. Sir Wm. Jones, a judge, buried.

Sergeant Grimston, Sergeant at Arms, buried.

Mr. Chamberlen the elder died.

18. Wm. Asply, bookseller, died.

August   Wm. Roberts, attorn. in Sussex, died.

23. Mr. Tutty, attorn. Comon Pleas, died.

27. Edw. Deeves, comon cryer, died.

Jo. Knight, churchwarden of St. Olaves in Old Jury, break his neck, and so died.

23. Dr. Vanderlosse, in Great Wood Street, died.

1. Mr. Ducane, in the Old Jury, buried.

4. Dorothy Coachman, daughter to Tilney Coachman, buried.

23. Anne Johnson, daughter to Mr. Bromhall, attorn. died.

Feb.   6. Mis Jumper, wife to Mr. Wm. Jumper, att. died.

11. My cozen, John Haselwood, died.

22. Stephen King, scrivener in Soper Lane, died.

March   4. Mis Johnson, widdow of Toby Johnson, died at Long-
field in Surrey.

8. Sir Miles Fleetwood, Receiver of the Court of Wards,
died.

19. Anthony Sharp, vintner, died.

1641.

29. Mr. Alexand. Bowling, scrivener behind the Exchange,
buried.

30. Mr. Silverlock, father to the wife of Mr. Robert Robinson, bur^d at Barnet.

27. Nath. Axtill, vintner in Newgate Market, died.

April   5. Roger Miller, attorn. and scrivener in Smithfield, died
sodenly.

17. Bird, a bookseller in St. Laurence Lane, died.

19. Mis Jerman, wife to Sergeant Jerman in Lad Lane,
died.

22. Sylvanus Scory died a prisoner in Wood Street Compter.

28. Mr. Wilkinson, my old honest taylor in Cony Hoop
Lane, died.

29. Mr. Skinner, our neighbour in ye Old Jury, died.

29. Mr. Anth. Low, councellor in St. Bartholomew's, brother to Arth. Low, sollicitor in the Excheq^r, died.

May   3. Wagstaff, brick layer in Aldersgate Street, buried.

9. Edw. Russell, Earle of Bedford, died of the small pox.

12. Tho. Earle of Stafford, beheaded on Tower Hill.

27. Math. Cradock, merchant, one of the Members of Parliament for ye city of London, died.

22. Ewyn Birch died, for whose death Mr. Morris and his
son Badger and Capt. Dalby were indighted and fined.

June 1. Mr. Phillips, of Clifford's Inne, died.
3. Tho. Bowes, of St. Martin's, died.
4. Sir Geo. Hastings, brother to the Earl of Huntingdon, died of the plague.
10. Wm. Drayton, of the Old Jury, died.
17 Stephen Buck, attorn. of Furnivall's Inne, died.
21. Mis Green, in the Old Jury, died.
27. Gregory, parish clerk of St. Olave's, Old Jury, died.
August 24. Parson Goodcole died.
Sept. 9. Mr. Orme, of Sir Pet. Osborn's office in the Exchequer, died, whose widow Mr. Wymonsold of the same office married.
Novem. 1. Rich. Smith, surgeon, died of the plague.
7. Geo. Johnson, in St. Laurence Lane, died.
11. Sir Christoph. Clitherow, alderman, died.
22. Robt. Heyman, mercer in Cheapside, died.
23. Mr. Chr. Pace, of the Court of Wards, died.
23. Mr. Tho. Lowes, of the Old Jury, died.
Decemb. 7. Hen. Patrickson, Silver Street, died.
16. Styward French, Under Shreiff, Midd'sex, died.
21. Mr. Edward Sherborn, secretary to the East India Company, and clerk of the Ordinance at the Tower, a courteous gentlm., died.
19. Tho. Sharples, a taylor, prisoner in Wood Street Compter (who had before gotten a great hurt by a fall down a paire of staires), died.
Febr. 10. John Masters, goldsmith at Fleet Bridg, died.
15. Mis Zouch, wife to Tho. Zouch, jacksmith, buried.
17. Sir Geo. Crook, judge of the King's Bench, died.
Mar. 24. Mr. John Crompton, secondary at Wood Street Compter, died at Reading.

1642.

April 9. Edw. Woodhouse, attorn. died at a tavern in Newgate Markett.

14. Mr. Wm. Jumper, attorn. died; buried ye 20th.

27. Old Mr. Hungate, in the Old Jury, died.

28. Mr. Thornton, of the Mayor's Court, and clerk of Butchers' Hall, buried.

30. The wife of Rowland Hughes, attorn. died.

May   2. Tho. Waters, notary publick, buried.

22. Mr. Almerye's second wife died.

Aug.   3. Rich. Smith, of Queenhith, serjeant at mace of Wood Street Compter, buried.

6. Mr. Edmonds, crowner, died sodenly.

Novem, 7. Sir Hen. Mountague, Earl of Manchest^r, Lord Privie Seale, and Lord President of the Councel, died.

7. Baron Page died sodenly.

Decem. 1. Robert Hughes, attorn. died.

17. John Wright, a yoeman of Wood Street Compter, died sodenly.

11. Arth. Yourth, clerk-sitter of ye Poultry, buried.

1643.

April   29. Gerard Herbert, alias Wright, of Hagerston, slayn by Slough, near Windsor, by some of the King's horse scouts.

May   16. Mr. Gibs, judg of the Sheriffs' Court for the Poultry Compter, buried.

16. Mis Webster, in Milk Street, died.

June   12. Mr. Josh. Shute, preacher in Lombard Street, died.

July   8. Sir Wm. Lamb, feodary, died in Fetter Lane.

11. Ambrose Mudford, attorn. Old Jury, buried.

12 Tho. Measure, a yoeman of the Compter, buried.

31. Captⁿ Wm. Barriff buried.

August 1. Edm. Wright, alderman, buried.

1. Lyddall, baker in the Old Jury, died.

3. Old Wm. Herbert, in Wood Street, died.

22. Mr. Randall, at ye Rose in Grub Street, died.

28. Old Mr. Woodhall, ye surgeon, died.

Sept.   8. My brother, Tho. Houlker, of King's Langly, died.

18. Captⁿ Geo. Mosse died of a wound received in a battle fought this month.

22. Mr. Pullen, of Hogsden, died.

28. Benjn. Blague, clerk-sitter, died.

28. Mr. Turner, clerk of Barber Surgeons' Hall, buried.

Mar.   13.* Leon. Lambard, founder in Lothbury, died.

14. Mr. Walthew, my Lo. Mayor's officer, died.

1644.

April   5. Mr. Foreby, attorn. buried.

5. Mr. Edw. Cook, apothecary in Fanchurch Street, buried.

May   13. John Law, of ye Old Jury, died of the plague.

16. Wm. Elliot, attorn. in Exchequer, buried.

16. John Leigh, eldest son to John Leigh, secondary of the Poultry Counter, died near Henley.

June   17. Mr. Leach, preacher at Bow in Cheapside, died.

22. Sir Edw. Deering, Kt. died of an apostume.

July   18. Tho. Waltham, Mr. Wymondsett's clerk, buried.

Aug.   8. John Huggon, attorn. died of a consumption.

Sept.   9. Fra. Hill, bookseller in Little Britain, died at Westminster.

14. Old Tho. Eagles, book-bearer in Guildhall, died.

14. Mr. Wicksted, attorn. in Lawrence Lane, died.

17. Martyn Lee, attorn. in Guildhall, died.

19. Mr. Fran. Quarles, a famous poet, died.

Octob.   Sir Hen. St. George, King at Arms, died at Oxon.

24. Sam. Dye died sodenly in Mr. Oglethorp's office.

Nov.   23. John Crompton the yonger, only son of John Crompton, Secondary, died about this time.

Decemb. 1. John Tymcock, in Wood Street, died.

11. Robt. Bateman, chamberlen, died.

18. The wife of Robt. Warner, chandler in Wood Street, died.

   23. Sir Alex^r Carey, Kt. beheaded on Tower Hill.

   28. Sir John Bancks, the King's attorney, died at Oxon.

March 14. Robt. Swaine, keeper of the Guild Hall, died of a
     burning feavor.

1645.

April 17. John Wells, attorn. of the Temple, died.

   22. Mr. Smithier, of the Prothonotory Office, died.

May 28. John Towse, alderman, died at Hampstead.

August 29. My cozen Jackson, minister, died in Essex.

Sept. 23. Will. Lambert, sergeant at mace, died of the plague.

   25. John Wells, painter by London Wall, died.

January 12. Robt. Barker, the King's printer, prisoner in the King's
     Bench for debt, buried.

Feb. 12. Mr. Romney, in Ironmonger Lane, died.

     Mr. Dun, M^r of the City Works, buried.

   11. My Lady Hatton's funerall.

1646.

April 17. Mis Crook, first wife of Andr. Crook, bookseller in
     Paul's church yard, died, a good woman.

May.   Mr. Pynder, surgeon in Smithfield, died.

June.   Chr. Parker, that married my wife's sister,

     Franes Edney died this month at the Barbados.

July   4. James Perrot, clerk-sitter, died.

August 24. Alderman Nich. Rainton died; buried 28.

   27. John, Mr. Matth. Barker's only son, of great hopes,
     buried.

   28. Mr. Fotherby, my Lord Mayor's officer, died.

   28. Hans Honger, alias John Huniades, the chymist with-
     out Algate, died.

   30. John Willis, of Kingsland, died.

Sept.   2. Mr. Atkinson, of Shoreditch, died of ye plague.

   12. Mr. Smithson, attorn. died at Chingford in Essex.

   14. Robt. Earl of Essex died.

Octob. 1. Wm. Young, chandler, within Aldersgate, a discreet juryman and Barba longa, died.

7. Lady Mary St. George, relict of Sir Hen. St. George, bur^d.

7. Leonard Skelton, in Little Wood Street, died.

14. Geo. Rookes, a staple merchant of no good report, buried.

19. Old Nich. King, of King's Langley, miller, buried.

Novem. 17. Lancelot Toppyn, bookseller in Little Britain, brother to Mis Bee, wife of Cornel Bee, died.

17. Ralpf Dell, of Stratford Bow, buried.

28. Geo. Lloyd, attorn. King's Bench, died.

Jan. 9. Mr. Barborne, merchant, buried.

Febr. 15. Mis Wright, wife to John Wright, brasier in the Old Jury, buried.

18. Mr. John Garway, merchant, died at Edmonton of ye plague.

21. Old Mr. Lewis, the mercenary preacher, buried.

26. My uncle Tho. Smith died at Stillingston in Dorsetshire, and buried March 2d.

Mar. 18. Mr. Geo. Duncomb, of Clifford's Inne, died in Surry.

Mr. Webb, joyner in Wood Street, died.

Tho. Smith, vintner, died.

Hen. Fetherston, stationer, died; buried 27.

1647.

March 26. Mis Seaman, wife to Tho. Seaman, attorn. in the Poultry, buried.

27. Sir Edw. Reeve, one of the justices of the Comon Pleas, died, with a good name.

April 6. Sir Hen. Pratt, alderman, died.

6. Ann Hutchinson, daughter to Mis Tench in the Poultry by her former husband Mr. Hutchinson, buried.

8. Mr. Hen. Haselfoot buried in Old Fish Street.

10. Old Mis Hudson, at the Mouth within Aldersgate, died.

13. Mr. Barker, in Coleman Street, died.

May   29. John Reynolds, of Lincoln's Inn, of the office of y^e
        Clerk of the Hamper, died.

24. Mr. Vdall, a sequestred minister, died.

24. Mr. Tho. Jumper, attorn. died.

24. Mr. Robt. Sadler, in Lombard Street, haberdasher,
    died.

June   5. Mr. Perry, bayliffe of the liberty of Westminster, died.

28. Mr. Rich. Antrobus, of Clifford's Inne, attorn. died of
    an apoplexie; buried July 1.

26. Chr. Turnor, attorn. of Bedford, died in London.

July   6. Geffry Ward, yoeman of the King's celler, died at
        Westminster of ye plague.

14. Day, a plumer, husband to my maid Katherin, died.

22. Wm. Butler, apothecary in Cornhill, died.

25. John Mills, late of ye Old Jury, died in Long Alley.

Aug.   1. Franc. Constable, bookseller at Westminster, died.

6. Jackson, Mr. Hebb's man, stationer in Paul's church
   yard, died of ye plague.

6. John, the 2d son of my daughter Hacker, died.

16. Gervas Partridge, attorn. died.

20. Roderick Powell died in Black Bull Yard in Cheap-
    side, where he dwelt.

My cozen, Tho. Bitcliffe the younger, died, son of Tho.
Bitcliffe, secondary of ye Poultry Compter.

31. Jonathan Hopkinson, bookseller wthout Algate, died.

Septem. 12. Old Fran. Wenham, butcher at Hagerston, died.

19. Mis Dickman, wife to John Dickman, apothecary, died.

23. Mr. Ballard, beadle of ye company of Ironmongers, and
    his son, both died of ye plague.

Octob.   2. Mr. Rich. Hull, silkman in Cheapside, died.

7. Mr. Brewster, stationer, buried.

8. Sir Richd. Gurney, late Lord Mayor, prisoner in the

Tower for his loyalty to ye King, buried in ye Old Jury.

12. Barthol. Partridg, attorn. a prisoner in Wood Street Compter, buried, dying of the plague.

Novemb. 11. Tho. Passand, a juryman of Langborn Ward, died.

13. Mr. Nath Hall, attorn. of the Excheq^r. died.

17. Mr. Ball, attorn. of ye Comon Pleas and Excheq^r. died.

17. Rich. Cartwright, bookseller in Duck Lane, died.

17. Mr. Smith, son in law to Rich. Cartwright, died.

Decemb. 31. Mis Bromhall, the relict of Mr. Lewis Bromhall, attorn. buried.

Jan. 6. Mr. Tho. Squier, once clerk-sitter in Wood Street Compter, buried in Paul's church.

7. Hen. Burton, the Independent minister, buried.^a

14. Mr. Hen. Medlicot buried at Richmond.

17. John Fanshaw, monier, died at Baulmes.^b

23. John Guy, a sergeant at Wood Street Compter, died.

Februar. Mr. Holborn, a noted lawyer, died about this time.

5. Rich. Whitacres, stationer, died.

16. Quarterman, sometime a brewer's clerk, the late independent marshall, died.

18. Mr. Pierse, my Lord Mayor's water bailiff, buried.

28. Maj^r Tho. Buxton, a grocer in Bucklersbury, buried.

March 10. Mr. Robt. Child, clerk of the Vintners' Company, and attorn. of the Mayor's Court, died.

1648.

April 3. Mr. Sam. Crisp and his wife, in Bread Street, killed in their bed by the fall of the floor of an upper room overladen.

---

^a Chalmers says he died on Jan. 7th.—ED.

^b Baulmes, or Balmes House, formerly in Shoreditch parish, but now in Hackney. The seat of the Welds, and afterwards of Sir George Whitmore, who died there in 1654.—ED.

3. Mis Powell, wife of John Powell of the Chamberlain's office, buried.

17. Mr. Ward, councellor of Gray's Inn, died.

17. Mr. Slinger, vintner at the Dogg at Westminster, died.

May 12. Mr. Robins, pewter, of St. Laurence by Guildhall, buried.

22. Mr. Matth. Jumper, of St. Martin's, died.

22. Mis Smith, wife to Hum. Smith, woolman, died of a timpany.

29. Robt. Blincoe, attorn. buried.

June. Neriah Mormay buried.

July. Mis Helmes, wife to John Helmes, attorn. died.

Mr. Fludd, (an honest Recusant,) my old acquaintance, about this time died.

30. Mr. John Parker, stationer, died.

Aug. 1. Mr. Wm. Hodges, attorn. died.

3. Justice Godbold died.

4. Alderman Robt. Backhouse died.

22. Mr. Aug. Garland the younger, his wife died of ye small pox in child-bed.

Sept. 5. Mr. Edw. Cropley, (who had fined for alderman,) died, very rich.

Octob. 26. Basil Niccols, clerk of the Haberdashers' Hall, buried.

26. Wm. Meredith, attorn. Guildhall, died.

27. Alderman John Warner, grocer, died.

28. Andr. Hebb, bookseller, died of a dropsie.

27. Mis Brock, Old Jury, died.

27. Tobias Dixon, mercer in Lombard Street, died.

Novemb. 1. Mr. Wm. Barker, attorn. died in debt.

19. Geo. Fisher, sergeant at Mace of Wood Street Compter, died.

22. Rich. Clutterbuck, stationer, died.

27. Mr. Tho. Stone, in Cateaton Street, a rich citizen, died.

23. Forth, an honest taylor in St. Martyn's, died.

29. The eldest daughter of Mr. John Niccols, keeper of Ludgate, buried.

30. Sir Geo. Garrett, alderman, died.

Decemb. 16. Sir Arthur Duck, D^r. of the Lawes, died sodenly in Chelsey Church.

16. Gough, vintner at the Castle in Paternoster Row, died.

21. Old Edw. Osbaldston, in the Poultry, buried.

20. Mr. Bolton, the elder, at Hogsdon, died.

22. Roger Snelson, dier, died.

23. Mr. Preston, mercer in Cheapside, died.

Jan. 30. King Charles beheaded at Westminster by his traiterous subjects.

Februar. 1. Sir Geo. Clark, alderman, died.

5. Mr. Clem. Mosse, Under Chamberlain, died.

March 5. Alderman Cordall, in Milk Street, died.

12. Mr. Rich. Aldworth, in Milk Street, buried.

17. Mr. Percival Pots, of the Exchange, died.

17. Tho. Frances, a goldsmith at Aldersgate, died.

22. Mr. Denington, attorn. died.

1649.

April 15. Mr. Rich. Alport, upholster in ye Poultry, died.

12. Sir John Gayer, late alderman, died.

16. Mr. Haunch, of All Hallows in ye Wall, died.

27. Rich. Hacker, eldest son of my daughter Martha Hacker, died at midnight.

May 2. Mr. Allen, our neighbor in Morefields, buried.

5. Dr. Soame, buried in Broad Street.

8. Mr. Ravenscroft, a chees-monger, in Cateaton Street, found drowned in a pond by Islington.

8. Mr. Keeling, councellor in Guildhall, died at his house in Hackney.

16. Dan. Frier, bookseller in Little Britain, buried.

17. Mr. Hobman, attorn. buried.

August 22. Dr. Rich. Holdsworth died.

Septem. 21. Mis Sadler, wife to Mr. Laur. Sadler, bookseller in Little Britain, buried.

21. Captn Massey, died at his house at Newington Green.

29. Mr. Ralph Sheppard's wife, died at Drapers' Hall.

Octob^r. 1. Pet. Pheasant, one of ye justices of ye Comon Pleas, died.

1. Hum. Smith, woolman, having broaken his legg wth a fall from his horse, fell into a feaver, and died.

17. Tho. Whitaker, son of Richard Whitaker, died.

8. Mr. Babington, merchant in St. Nich. Lane, died.

12. Cuthb. Hacket. keeper of ye Poultry Compter, died.

30. Mr. Willm. Bowyer, vintner in ye Poultry, died.

Decemb. 16. Mr. Rich. Kilvert, died sodenly.

John Harison, grocer in Cateaton Street, died.

7. Elias Day, cook in ye Old Jury, died.

19. Steph. Sedgwick, brewer at Fleet Bridge, buried.

Jany. 23. Phil. Herbert, Earl of Pembrook and Mongomery, Lord Chamberlain, died.

Mr. Gibbons, attorn. of Coventry, died.

29. Mr. Gwyn, of Furnivals Inn, died.

30. Tho. Zouch, jack maker in Gutter Lane, died.

29. Fran. Kemp, attorn. Fleet Street, died.

30. Alderman Hoyle, of York, hanged himself.

31. Edw. Gilbert, clerk of the Dyers' Company, died, and bur^d Feby 2nd.

Februar. 19. Robt. Wilson, alderman, one of the sheriffs of London, died, and buried Mar. 5.

19. Mis Middleton, in the Compter Alley, in Poultry, died.

Mar. 8. Mr. Beaumond, attorn. in Wood Street, died.

13. Mr. Halhead, one of the commissioners of the city, died. at Northampton, and his wife at London on Munday following.

19. Mis Forth, lately married to Spatchurst, a taylor, died in child bed.

22. Mr. Torshell, preacher at Criplegate, died; was son of Mᵗˢ Torshell, a midwife.

1650.

March   25. Mr. Wm. Wild, vintner in Bread Street, died; father to Sir Wm. Wild, now recorder.

30. Mr. Worsley, father to Mr. Tho. Worsly, clerk of the papers, died at Tibbolds.

April   2. Walter Monck, milliner at the long shop in Cheapside, died.

10. Wm. Small yᵉ yonger, in Aldersgate Street, attorn. died.

13 Mr. Richd. Leigh, merchᵗ in St. Ellen's, died.

18. Sir Sim. Dews, yᵉ antiquary, died.

25. Mr. Jefferson, alehouse keeper in Morefields, died.

25. Fran. Lawrence, sollicitor in Aldermanbuy, buried.

May   20. Bernard Ostler, scrivener in the Old Jury, died of a blow on his head with a wine pint pot given by Mr. Bovey, for which he was afterwards indicted, but acquitted.

22. Tho. Samon, mercer, died.

June   28. Capt. John Ven, a member of Parliament for the city of London, died.

July   15. Mr. Docrey, brasier in yᵉ Old Jury, buried.

30. Mr. Fisher, barber and bookseller in Old Baily, died.

August   13. Hamond Thurston, mercer, St. Mich. Quern, buried.

16. Cozen Elizab. Hazelwood, in Aldersgate parish, buried.

17. Sam. Cartwright, bookseller, died.

Aug.   17. Lanc. Lancaster, our exigent writer, died.

18. Baron Rigby, ⎰takeing an infection in their circuit at
19. Baron Gates, ⎱ Croydon; the High Sheriff of Surry also died.

22. Coll. Euseb. Andrews beheaded on Tower Hill for his loyalty.

27. Manesty Reeve died.

Sept.   4. Mr. Staple, schoolmaster in Grub Street, died.

8. The Lady Elizabeth, daughter to the late King, died at Carisbrook Castle.

Decemb. 25. Andr. Boaa, turnkey of Newgate, died.

Januar.   Mr. Tho. Watson, attorn. King's Bench, died.

22. Sir Wm. Acton, alderman, Kt. and Bart. died.

Febr.   18. My good old mother Mis Martha Smith died at Lime's End, and buried at Lellingston.

Mar.   4. Sir Hen. Hyde beheaded in Cornhill, agst Exch.

Wm. Pragell, fishmonger, died about this time.

1651.

Mar.   26. My son in law Wm. Hacker murthered near Franckfort in Germany.

27. Mr. Tisdale, councellor of Gray's Inne, murthered in his chamber.

29. Capt. Brown Bushell beheaded on Tower Hill.

Apr.   8. Sir Wm. Beecher, Clerk of ye Councell, died at Putney; was there buried.

25. Mr. Taylor, brewer in Old Street, died.

26. Robt. Gibson, sergeant at mace, died.

May   3. Mr. Hen. Cogan, Controller of ye Mint, died.

June   8. Nevil Cradock, attorn. Clifford's Inne, died.

  •   12. Mr. Tho. Ken, of Furnivall's Inne, ye Sheriff's attorney-accomptant, died.

13. Griffin Morris and Mr. Ken buried.

Mr. Wm. Taylor, at the Hen and Chickens in Paternoster Row, mercer, died.

July   15. Ralph Hartley, scrivener in Cornhill, died.

21. Eliz. my son John's child, died of convulsion fits.

29. Young Ben. Wallinger, killed falling from a horse.

25. My aunt Jodrell, buried at Shillingstone, in Dorsetshire.

August   Mr. Robotham, upholsterer in the Poultry, buried.

22. Christoph. Love, a preacher, and Mr. Gibbons, beheaded on Tower Hill.

26. Abr. Chamberlen, merchant at St. Mary Axe, died.

29. Tho. Smith of Furnival's Inne, buried.

Sept.   10. Mr. Mich. Gardner, vintner, died.

11. Mr. Noble, a gardiner in Shordich, died.

28. Tho. Bancks, attorn. in Staple's Inn, died.

28. Tho. Witherings, post master, died sodenly.

Octob^r.   1. Gilbt. Harison, once alderman and sheriff, now chamberlain of London, died poore.

1. Coll. Blundell, in Milk Street, died.

10. Young Chancey of Chigwell, rob'd and kill'd.

10. Robt. Broom, ironmonger in Cheapside, died.

12. Joseph Lanman, attorn. died.

11. Mis Llewellen, wife of Wm. Llewellen, keeper of the Guildhall, buried ye 15th; Mr. Llewellen was since an alderman of London.

17. John Blackmore, silversmith, died.

24. John Read, in St. Laurence Lane, died.

12. Ralph Hayes in Cornhill, serjeant at mace, died.

Novem.   6. Josias Tully, of the seal office, died.

10. Ben. Clark, attorn. King's Bench, died.

Decemb. 16. Mr. Roger Drake, mercer in Cheapside, buried.

Januar.   1. John Trevillian, goldsmith, once a sergeant, died.

6. Mr. Hobson of ye Petty Bagg, died at his house in Bushey.

12. Mr. Ogliander, linen draper, Cheapside, died.

13. Rich. Coates, city printer, died.

14. Katherin, 2nd wife to Mr. Wm. Newbold, Old Jury, seipsam (pro dolor) laqueo strangulavit.

17. Geo. Snaith, once servant to ye A.Bp. Canterbury, died.

19. The wife of Braford, a porter in ye postern, murthered her owne infant, for which she was afterwards hanged.

31. Mr. Walter Marks, attorn. Mayor Court, died.

Feb.   6. Capt. Geares died.

26. Mr. Dun, surgion, in Guildhall Yard, died.

Mar.   2. Our neighbor old Mr. Marshall, ropemaker, in More-fields, died.

1652.

Mar.   28. Mr. Louing, an apothecary, Little Britain, died.

29. Mr. Robt. Carpenter, clerk of y⁰ papers of y⁰ Poultry Compter, died.

Apr.   10. Mⁱˢ Fletcher, wife of James Fletcher, of St. Laurence parish, died.

13. Mr. Moore, turnkey, at Ludgate, died.

16. Mr. Cornwall, attorn. Comon Pleas, died at Reading; being dead he was so extreamly fatt as he weighed 392ˡᵇ.

May   10. Sam. Harfleet, once an attorn. clerk at Guildhall, died in Newgate, wher he was clerk.

14. Mr. Granwell, buried at Stratford, Bow.

June   4. Tho. Dainty, at the Jack a Napes in Cheapside, died.

July   17. Edward Earl of Dorset died.

17. Mr. Batt, clerk of the papers, died at Mr. Sondies in Cheapside.

27. Dominick Turner, vintner, died.

27. Mr. Powell, vintner in Fleet Street, died.

27. Mr. Thurburn, inkeeper wᵗʰout Bishopgate, died.

August   10. Old Ralph Sheppard, beadle of Draper Hall, buried.

11. Mⁱˢ Bide, wife to alderman Bide, died.

11. Mr. Fran. West, Lieutᵗ. of the Tower, died.

16. Old Mⁱˢ Tho. Crowder, in Shorditch, buried.

17. Old Mr. Jekyll, attorn. King's Bench, died.

Sept.   11. John Wilcox, sergeant, Wood Street, died.

13. Isaac Rott, attorn. died at Stratford Bow.

15. Geo. Broom, attorn. King's Bench, died.

19. Coll. Robt. Manwering died in Grubstreet.

23. Mr. Aspley, comfit maker, died, who married ye widd. of Laur. Hill, grocer.

Octr. 4. Rich. Kilborn, attorn. died.

8. Mr. Grave,* the Arabick scholler, died.

22. Ham. Dakyn, a constable of Islington, murthered, and there buried.

Nov. 6. Sir Nath. Brent, Aldersgate Street, died.

8. Mr. Smithier, scrivener in Ivy Lane, died.

Dec. 3. Mr. Christmas, merchant in Basinghall, died.

17. Mr. Nicols, clerk of Haberdashers' Hall, buried.

16. Jonathan Blinco, attorn. died.

17. Mr. Rich. Sedgwick, in Broad Street, died.

19. Tho. Herrick, son of Mr. Nich. Herrick, died.

22. Anne, wife of my brother Walter Smith, died at Low Leighton, leaving behind her xi. little ones, and was buried with her infant Harry ye 27th.

Decem. 22. Mr. Hide, a glasier in Little Britain, killed by a fall of a ladder, buried.

24. John Daves, Old Jury, broaker, a prisoner in Ludgate, buried in St. Olave's, Old Jury; his son Tho. Daves, a bookseller, was afterwards an Alderman and Lord Mayor of London, enriched by the legacy of Hugh Audley.

Januar. 20. Geo. Norman, sergeant at Wood Street, died.

24. Mr. Heath, surgeon in Coleman Street, buried.

27. John Davenport, sergeant in Wood Street, died.

Febr. 5. Robt. Greenhill, attorn. Little Old Baily, died.

6. Mis Mountague, wife to Mr. Mountague, bookseller in Little Brittain, died in child-bed.

6. Mr. Wm. Vaughan, Old Jury, died, buried 24th.

16. Mr. Watterhouse, in Cheapside, died.

---

* This was John Greaves, best known as a mathematician, and as the author of " Pyramidologia, or a Description of the Pyramids of Egypt." 8vo. Lond. 1646.

20. Old Mis Jaggard (a good woman) died.

22. Sir Peter Richault died, buried at Aylesford in Kent.

March   3. Mr. Methiwold (sometime sword-bearer) died.

7. Arth. Knight, hanged in Covent Garden, (where his father, a haberdasher of hatts, dwelt,) for killing one Furnival; his mother was sister to Mis Horrick in the Old Jury.

19. Mr. Berridg, in Little Britain, buried.

1653.

March   27. Mr. John de Gret, brewer in Red Cross Street, died sodenly in his bed at night, having been at chur. y^t day.

27. Mr. Tho. Croft, in Barbican, my sister Edney's first husband, died.

28. Old Mr. Whiteker, the wax choferer for the Seales at Westminster, died.

April   4. Mr. Morecroft, apothecary in Fleet Street, buried.

14. John Hinson, bookbinder in Gutter Lane, buried.

14. Mr. Smallwood, clockmaker in Lothbury, died, and buried the 18th.

17. Mr. Vnderhill, in Cannon Street, died.

18. Mis Banister, in Lad Lane, and her daughter Pointer, buried both in one grave.

26. Hugh Lewis, goldsmith in Little Britain, hanged at Tyborn, for receiving and concealing stolen plate.

27. Simon Hide, my Lord Mayor's officer, died.

May   10. Mr. Wm. Morris (my landlord at Hagerston) died.

10. Mr. Goddard, of St. Gregories, died.

17. Sergeant John Green died in Fleet Street, buried in the country.

17. Mr. Kemm, bookseller in Duck Lane, died.

19. Mr. Cristoph. Meredith, bookseller in Paul's Church Yard, partner with Mr. Phil. Stephens, died.

23. Mr. Hull, pewterer, died sodenly.
24. Anthony Brown, attorn. Com'on Pleas, died.
24. Geo. Dakyn, attorn. King's Bench, died.
28. Mr. Attkinson, turnkey of yᵉ Poultry Compter, died.

June   3. Mr. Low, a Blackwell Hall man, buried.
9. My cozen Elizab. Smith, eldest daughter of my brother Walter Smith, aged Novemb. last 19 years, died, and buried yᵉ 20ᵗʰ at St. Bride's.
14. Geo. Whiteker, my clerk, died at his father's.

July   6. John Bisse, bookseller, died.
27. Capt. Jones, our neighbor in Morefields, died.

August   4. Mr. Flesher, in Little Brittain, died.
10. My son Richard, aged (Sept. 14 next) 16 years, died, and buried the 12ᵗʰ.
11. Robert Worden (alias Fidler), a waterman, drowned below Bridge about this time.
12. Wm. Low, the comon hangman, died about this time.
7. Flint, an attorn. at Barnard's Inne, hanged himself.
26. Mr. Gibson, in yᵉ Compter Alley in Poultry, died.
29. Mark Ewer, in Ironmonger Lane, buried.
30. Mr. Ferryman, haberdasher small wares in the Poultry, died.

Sept.   1. Mr. Claxton, in Cheapside, died.
1. Pet. Haywood, of the Excheqʳ, died.
2. Dr. de Neue died sodenly at All Hallows in the Wall.
5. Mr. Rainsford, woollen draper, died.
11. John Crosse, an honest butcher in Newgate markett, died, well known to my bro. Walt. his customer.
9. John Fosbrook, Mr. Corn. Bee's man, died at Amsterdam, a good servant but a bad husband.
9. Dr. Rant, physician, died, who attempting to creep to bed to Mˡˢ Bennett, lost his credit and his purchase.
25. Mr. Wheelock, an Arabick reader, buried.

28. Old Ned. Worsley, Alderman Kendrick's Clerk, buried.

Sept^r.   Edm. Vnderwood, attorn. Comon Pleas, died the last
Vacation, in Lime Street.

Oct^r.   3. Phillips, my Lord Mayor's officer, died poor.

6. Mr. Cox, an able sollicitor, died.

7. Mr. Whitcher, in Middle Row, in Holborn, my man
George's father, died, buried ye next day.

8. Robt. Pickering, attorn. Clifford's Inne, died.

12. Mr. Hamond, a cook in Bow Lane, died.

22. Fran. Manesty, scrivener in Cornhill, died.

22. Mr. Chamberlen, mercer in Cheapside (partner wth
Mr. Pettit), died at Greenwich.

Novem.   5. Old Elias Buckmaster, of Chipperfield, died.

15. Mis Robinson, wife of Mr. Hum. Robinson, bookseller,
buried.

12. Mr. Marriot, attorn. of the Uper Bench, died.

12. Abr. Vandecouter, a Dutch mercht. died.

16. John Baker, bookseller, died.

17. Mis Flud, once a cake maker at Hogsden, in Morefields, died.

25. Mr. Bowyer, in Horse Shoe Alley, Morefields, buried.

21. My cozen Tho. Houlker's wife buried, a chandler's
daughter in Chancery Lane.

21. Mr. John Squier, once minister of Shoreditch,* buried.

25. Old Marriot, of Gray's Inn (ye great eater), buried.

26. John Pope, of Clifford's Inn, attorn. buried.

30. Mr. Robt. Bowyer, merchant in Old Jury, buried.

Decem.   1. Jaspar Chapman, grocer in Milk Street, buried.

16. Old Dr. Googe, buried in his church at Black-ffryers.

18. Kellam Smith (once a sergeant at mace), died at Litchfield, and was there buried, Decem. 24.

---

* He was sequestered from his vicarage, by a Committee of the House of Commons, in
1642.—ED.

29. Michael Sparke, bookseller, buried.
31. Mr. Johnson, the chymist, buried.

Januar. 5. Old Mr. Banister, in Lad Lane, died.

Jany. 9. Rich. Best (a packer), died in Lombard Street.

16. Mr. Rich. Core, chandler in Old Jury, his only sonn buried.
26. John Monger, prothonotary at Guild Hall, died, buried 28.
27. Mich. Smith, a yeoman of Wood Street Compter, buried.
31. Ralph Hanson, clerk of the Ironmongers, buried.

Febr. 8. James Pryn, attorn. Furnival's Inn, died in Hillary Term.

16. Edm. Smith, dr. physick, died of a pleuresie in Shoe Lane.
21. Mr. Durham, proctor at Dr. Comons, buried, father to our neighbor Mr. Billingsly.
22. James Pychley, clerk of the exigents, died in Wood Street.
24. Alex. Rosse, a Scotchman, a good schollar and a writer of many tracts, died.*

Mar. 12. Mr. Walker, preacher at All Hallows in ye Wall, died.
18. Mr. Justice Jermyn died.

1654.

April 18. Mr. John, Mr. Ladore's man, died.
20. Mr. Godfrey Maydwell, attorn. buried.

May 9. Mary Ladore, daughter of Pet. Ladore, buried.
16. Old Mr. Rowland Wilson, vintner, died.
18. Rich. Meredith, attorn. Wood Street, died.

---

* Butler records his name in Hudibras,

" There was an ancient sage Philosopher
Who had read Alexander Rosse over."

Evelyn, in his Diary, says, " 1649, July 11, came to me old Alexander Rosse, the divine, historian, and poet."—ED.

19. Mr. Simonds, the printer, died.
17. Mr. Scattergood, vintner at the Miter, Cheapside, died.

June 1. Tho. Lethbridge, attorn. Clifford's Inn, died.
7. Mⁱˢ Myn, wife to Rich. Myn, bookseller in Little Brittain, died.
13. Rich. Swinglehurst, clerk to the East India Company, died in St. Mary Axe.
25. Mrs. Tuke, wife to Old Parson Tho. Tuke, in yᵉ Old Jury died, buried yᵉ 27.

July 1. Young John Crompton, grandchild to Mr. John Crompton, secondary (by his son John), buried.
10. Mr. Vowell, school mʳ at Islington, hanged at Charing Cross for his loyalty to yᵉ king.
10. Mr. Gerard, for the same, beheaded on Tower Hill.
10. A seruant of yᵉ Portugall ambassador (an Englishman), hanged at Tyborn for killing one Mr. Greenway on yᵉ New Exchange.
27. Mr. Corn. Bee's wife, Little Brittain, died, buried Aug. 1.
30. Walter Hayes, dyer, died, buried Aug. 3.

Aug. 5. Old Mr. Marshall, at the Arrow in Finsbury, died.
12. Mⁱˢ Hutchinson, the relict of Mr. Tho. Hutchinson, vintner in Aldersgate Street, buried.
12. Mr. Beauchamp, in Little Brittain, died.
16. Mr. Hook (our neighbor in Morefields) died.
15. Hen. Bourcher, Earl of Bath, died.
17. Mr. Francklyn, a warder at yᵉ Tower, my old schoolfellow at Abingdon, died.
18. Mrs. Grice, in Aldersgate Street, buried.
21. Mr. Vaughan, in Cheapside, goldsmith, died.
22. Mr. Hadley, in St. Laurence Lane in yᵉ Jury, buried.

Sept. 9. Deputy Holliday, of Gracechurch, inkeeper, died.
18. Mr. Andrews, goldsmith, Cheapside, buried.
21. Lo. Bramston, late Lord Ch. Justice, buried.
20. Dr. Wynnyff, Bp. of Lincoln, died.

22. Mr. Burges, in Upper Morefields, by the Pope's Head, died.

26. Mr. Viccars, at yᵉ Bull at Hogsden, died about this time.

Octʳ. 6. Dr. Bastwick, physician, buried.

20. Goodwife Allen, in yᵉ Old Jury, died.

Ozias Churchman, woolen draper in Watlingstreet, died.

Nov. Capt. Lane, haberdasher in Friday Street, died.

9. Tho. Price, son, chandler (once serjeant at mace), of yᵉ Old Jury, buried.

13. Andr. Cater, Coleman Street, woolman, buried.

13. Mr. Conn, scrivener in Cornhill, died.

15. Mr. Christmas, stone-cutter in yᵉ Postern, buried.

20. Mr. Tho. Bucher, pewterer wᵗʰin Aldersgate, buried.

23. Mr. Speering, counceller at Guildhall, died.

23. Mr. Grinder in yᵉ Poultry, buried.

30. Mr. John Selden yᵉ antiquary died; buried Dec. 14.

29. Sir Chr. Yelverton, Kt. died.

30. Old Mr. Page, Mʳ in Chancery, died.

Decem. 8. Matth. Jones, a clerk of the Poultry comptʳ, died in Old Street.

10. Wm. Meredith, Mr. Codington's clerk, died.

10. Hen. Nailor, a messenger of yᵉ Poultry Compt. died.

12. Fra. Pattys, glasier (a juriman), Lumber st. died.

12. Sir Geo. Whitmore, once Lord Mayor, died.

14. Mr. Hen. Jackson (my worthy friend) buried.

15. Dr. Moulshaw, physician in Aldersgate Street, died.

16. Rich. Major, vintner at yᵉ 3 Tons by Guildhall, died intestate.

29. Wm. Barwick, Mr. Houson's clerk, attorn. died.

Janu. 4. Robt. Lowther, mercht. in Lothbury, died.

12. Chr. Walker, councellʳ. in St. John Street, died, a stiring industrious man.

Febru. 1. Justice Geo. Long at Clerkenwell, died.

8. Mr. Wm. Bevis of the Tower, died.

23. Mrs. Osbaldston, widdow in ye Poultry, buried.

March   4. Conway, bag bearer of ye Exchequer, died in Ivy Lane.

16. Mr. Boyden, bookseller by ye Tower, died.

1655.

March   29. Sir Theodor. Mayern, the King's physician, aged 82 years, buried.

29. Paul Isaack in Aldermanbury, merchant, buried.

29. Du. of Richmond and Lennox died.

April   3. John Shuckforth, attorn. buried at Croydon.

8. Mr. Pemberton, preacher at St. Foster's, died.

13. Mr. Taylor, mercht. in Coleman Street, died.

11. Rich. Lapley, mercht. died.

16. Mr. Martin Brown, surgeon, died.

May   5. John Smith ye elder, shopkeeper in St. Martin's Le Grand, buried.

6. My only and eldest son John Smith, beloved of all men (proh dolor), died at Micham in Surry, and buried in Lond. May 9, at St. Giles, Cripplegate.

June   4. Mr. Tombes (sometime Sir Paul Pindar's servant) hanged himself.

July   13. Old Mr. Wm. Small, attorn. died about this time.

24. Mr. John Lamot, Dutch mercht. buried.

25. Mr. Nich. Wem, attorn. Furnival's Inn, died.

Aug.   1. James Fletcher, by St. Laurence Church, Guildhall, foreman of Criplegate Jury, died; buried 14.

8. Hen. Colborn, scrivener in Walbrook, died.

11. M^{ls} Jerom, wife to John Jerom, attorn. died.

14. Mr. Rich. Edwards, apothecary in Cheapside, died.

18. Alice, daughter to my coz. John Clutterbuck, my god-daughter, buried.

22. Walter Hillary, attorn. Excheq^r. of Clifford's Inn, died.

Octob.   19. Mr. Billingsley at ye Pipe Office and Excheq^r. died.

24. Dr. Winston, phisitian, died.

Novem. 20. Auditor Tooke in Aldersgate Street, died.

29. Tho. Nevet, goldsmith in Lombard Street, buried.

29. Abr. Heylin, bodies maker, Bow Lane, died.

Decem. 23. John Taylor, sergeant, Poultry Compter, buried.

27. Mis Woollaston, wife to Hen. Woollaston, haberdasher in Lombard Street, buried.

28. Mis Broome, wife to Mr. Tho. Broome, councellor in Bassinghall Street, buried.

31. Nich. Walgrave, an honest serjeant of ye Poultry, buried.

31. Old Tho. Aram, late a yeoman of ye Poultry Compter, aged 100 years, buried.

Januar. 18. Elizab. daughter of Matt. Barker, attorn. in Wood Street, died.

20. James Glasbrook, that once kept ye White Lyon alehouse in Guildhall Yard, after fined for alderman; lastly died sodenly in Little Britain, at Dr. Micklewait's door.

20. Mr. Geo. Dixon, son of Mr. Robt. Dixon, of King's Langley, died in ye Strand.

25. Edw. Buckle, of ye Chamberlain's Office, died.

31. Walter Melton, pewterer in Lothbury, buried.

Feb. 4. Mr. Vines, preacher at Laurence Jury, having ye day before preached and given the sacrament, died this morning.

10. John Waterson, once a bookseller, died.

March 20. Alice, daughter of my son John, died; buried 21.

22. Phill. Darrell, auditor, buried at St. Giles, Criplegate.

22. James Usher, abp. of Armagh in Ireland, died at Rigate, aged 80 years; buried Apr. 17 following.

22. Tho. Harper, printer in Little Britain, buried.

1656.

April 2. Mrs. Fawne, wife to Capt. Luke Fawne, bookseller in Paul's Church Yard, buried.

15. Mr. Rob. Mitchell, Controuller of yᵉ Chamber (once Town Clerk) died, Mr. Avery succeeding him.

17. Mˡˢ Wells, wife to Mr. Wells, our neighbor in Gun Alley, died.

18. Sir Wm. Sidley died of yᵉ meazils; his funerall this day, carried into Kent from London.

April   24. Mˡˢ Dixon, of King's Langley, a wise, and well-governed gentlewoman, buried.

25. John Burdet, serjeant at yᵉ Poultry Compter, buried.

May   16. Coll. Harrison, wollen draper, buried.

21. Mr. Hales, prebend of Windsor, buried at Lauley by Windsor.ᵃ

June   7. Mˡˢ Louing, in Little Britain, yᵉ apothecary's relict, buried.

10. Mˡˢ Beauchamp, in Little Brittain, died; buried 17.

17. Hannam, a notorious thief, who often had broke prison, at last was taken, and hanged in Smithfield.

20. Mr. Piggot, grocer in St. Clement's Lane, buried.
Tho. Hutchinson, Esqr. once a vintner at the Sun in Aldersgate Street, died.

23. Mr. Justice Aske died.

24. Old Mr. Ridgley, phisition, died.
Old Wm. Carpenter, brewer wᵗʰout Algate, sometime alderman's deputy there, died.

25. Lady Vyner, wife to Sir Tho. Vyner, alderman, died.

July   4. My cozen Tho. Clutterbuck's wife, a good woman, in letting of her blood died; buried 10.

4. James Kirk, merchant, died.

7. Mˡˢ Huggins, late wife of John Huggins, attorn. in Wood Street, buried.

26. Mr. John Reading, secondary at Wood Street, died at Hammersmith; buried in London 26.

ᵃ This was John Hales, usually distinguished by the appellation of "the ever memorable." Chalmers says "he was buried according to his own desire in *Eton church-yard,* where a monument was erected over his grave by Mr. Peter Curwan."—Ed.

Sir Robt. Berkley, late Justice of ye King's Bench, died this Vacation.

30. Hen. Rolls, late Ch. Justice of ye King's Bench, died.

30. Jo. Wright, brasier Old Jury, died at Low Laighton.

31. My cozen Tho. Houlker died at King's Langley, and buried there Aug. 1.

August 3. Mr. Singleton, clerk of ye Mercers' Company, died.

9. James Davis, bookseller in Little Brittain, buried.

18. Mr. Bagott, brewer, son in law to Mr. Newbold, died insolvent.

20. John Harvey, a juryman in Coleman Street, died.

28. Mis Morgan, wife to Ellis Morgan, bookseller in Little Brittain, died.

Septem. 1. Dr. How, phisitian in Milk Street, died.

6. Mr. Edm. Demy, of Clifford's Inn, died at Chigwell.

8. Bp. Jos. Hall died, *plenus dierum, plenus virtutum.*

24. Tho. Price, junr. chandler in Old Jury, died.

27. Tho. Symonds, gentl. Bishopgate, died prisoner in ye Fleet.

Octr. 5. Rich. Mearing, next ye Compter in Wood Street, died.

10. Alderman Edmonds, died in Aldermanbury.

10. David Edwards, wollen draper in Cannon Street, hurt by ye fall of a cart wheel, wch bruised his thigh.

15. Jo. Day, in Fanch Church Street, a merchant broker, buried.

Nov^br. 27. Mr. Farrar, in Little Morefields, died sodenly.

28. Sir Robt. Shirley, prisoner in ye Tower, died of the small pox.

Decem. 1. Mr. Thankfull Frewin's corps (sometime clerk to Tho. Lord Coventry) carried through London to be interred in Sussex: he was brother to ye A.Bp. of York.

11. Robt. Bostock, died sodenly in ye Street at Banbury; was formerly a bookseller in Paul's churchyard.

12. Mr. Jennings, a smith, died sodenly in Wood Street.

28. Mr. John Walters, clerk of ye Drapers and clerk of the Mayor's Court, died; buried Jan. 6.; a charitable, honest, good man.

 Mr. Cory, a prothonotary of the Comon Pleas, died about this time.

Janua. 7. Mr. Kitchell, attorn. Clement's Inn, buried.

7. Mr. Horsnell, attorn. Comon Pleas, buried.

8. Matthias Abbot, habat. Cheapside, died at Norwich.

13. Mis Codington, wife to Mr. Wm. Codington, in Bow Lane, died; buried ye 16.

14. Alderman Edw. Sleigh died; buried 29.

12. Nathan Stirrop, in Aldersgate Street, gentleman, late of Sir Miles Fleetwood's office, died; buried 16.

21. Old Matth. Hancock, attorn. died.

Febr. 4. Nathan^{ll} Thorold, Marshall of ye Exchequer, buried.

March 6. Sir Tho. Trevor, once Baron Excheq^r, died about this time.

17. Mis Tench, wife to Mr. Geo. Tench in ye Poultry, died; buried ye 20.

17. Coll. Vaughan, leather seller, Cornhill, buried.

20. Mr. Tho. Man, haberdasher at London Ston, died.

22. Mr. Edlyn, preacher at Basinghall church, died.

1657.

March 27. Old Mr. Hen. Ayres, in Wood Street, died; buried 31.

April 22. Mr. James Cranford, preacher at St. Christoph^{rs}, died.

23. Mr. Fletcher, vpholster in Cornhill, buried.

May 4. Mr. Pulleyn, Remembrancer, died sodenly at Reading.

28. Mr. Hogan Hovel's funerall at Grocers' Hall.

20. The wife of Mr. John Nichols, keeper of Ludgate, died at her house in Wales.

June 2. Dr. Harvey, an old learned phisician,[a] died.

---

[a] Dr. William Harvey, who first discovered the circulation of the blood.—ED.

4. Rob. Vallence, once living wthout Bishopgate, inn-keeper, died at his house in Clerkenwell.

17. Hen. Crone, sen^r. vintner, died sodenly at Barn Elms.

27. Nich. Towers, one of ye sheriffs of York city, died in his sherivalty.

July   10. Old Mr. Geo. Tench, in the Poultry, not long outliving his wife, buried in ye Poultry church.

22. Fran. Newton, attorn. in Paul's Alley in Red Cross Street, buried.

Aug^t.   5. Mr. Ward, vintner at ye Half Moon, Aldersgate Street, died.

28. Mr. Blackwell, linen draper, Newgate Market, buried.

28. John Lilburn, a busie man, died at Eltham, and buried in the new church yard by Bedlam ye 31, accompa-nied wth his fellow Quakers.[a]

31. Nath. Butler hanged in Cheapside for killing a young man his bed-fellow in Milk Street.

Mr. Hen. Cutts, attorn. of the Comon Pleas, died this Vacation.

Mr. Anth. Wright, attorn. of the Comon Pleas, died about the same time at Padington.

Sept.   2. Mr. May, attorn. Ld Mayor's Court, buried.

9. Mis Huson, wife to Mr. Wm. Huson attorn. buried.

13. Old Mr. Tho. Tuke, once minister at St. Olave's in ye Old Jury, buried at ye new chappell by the new mar-kett place in Lincoln's Inn Fields.

14. Mr. Langley, an able school m^r of Paul's, died.

28. Mr. Andr. Drybutter, in Old Jury, died.

Octob^r.   13. Rich. Overton, habd. Cheapside, buried.

13. Hen. Dickman, apothecary, died,

23. Fran. Mosse, scrivener in Cornhill, buried.

Novem.   24. Mr. Rainsford, mercer in Cheapside, died.

---

[a] Four thousand persons are said to have attended his burial.—ED.

Mr. Tho. Leigh, younger brother of Mr. Edward Leigh
secondary, about this time died in Staffordshire, and
his only daughter and child at Greenwich.

Decem. 4. John Hurst, late sergeant at mace at Wood Street,
died.

15. Alderman Estwick died.

17. Mr. Janson's corps carried out of Finsbury into Northamptonshire to be buried.

22. Moses Dannet, at yᵉ Dagger in Foster Lane, buried.

Januar. 1. Mr. Bonnett of the Pipe Office buried.

9. Adam Kent, attorn. Clifford's Inn, died.

19. Alderman Wm. Underwood, in Bucklersbury, his
funerall.

Febr. 19. Tho. Downs, stationer, died, buried 22.

Dan Reading, attorn. at Clifford's Inn, brother to
secondary Reading, died in Hillary Term.

March 16. Gerard Carpenter, attorn. Guildhall, died in Wood
Street, buried 20.

Roger Price, wollen draper, died at his house in
Buckinghamshire.

21. Mr. Carter, preacher at St. Giles, Criplegate, died.

1658.

March 26. Nathan Wright, merchᵗ in Mark Lane, buried.

April 9. Sam. Clutterbuck, clerk, my brother-in-law, died this
day, being Good Friday, at Dunton.

16. Mr. Langham, by the posthouse, brother to alderman
Langham, died ; buried 22.

18. Robt. Earle of Warwick died.

19. Mr. John Holt, attorn. at Guildhall, having first
secured his place to Mr. Aires, died in Milk Street;
buried in Essex yᵉ 27.

21. Geo. Latham, bookseller in Paul's Church Yard, died.

26. Tho. Hardesty, bookseller in Duck Lane, a poore man,

willingly leaping out of his window into the street
3 stories high, broke his neck and so died.

26. Sir John Woollaston, alderman, died.

29. My brother Edw. Smith died at my house in Morefields; buried 30.

May   8. Mr. Luggard, bookseller at ye Postern by ye Tower,
buried.

10. Anth. Peniston, once a juror in Lombard Street, died
at his house now in Aldersgate.

11. John Wright, bookseller in ye Old Bayly, buried.

16. Alderman Nathan Tomse, died of ye falling sickness;
but ill the day before.

4. Old John Grove, plumer in Lad Lane, died.

June.   Mr. Geo. Haughton, apothecary, died.

3. Mr. Abbot, scrivener in Cornhill, died, *dives et probus.*

4. Old Mis Watkins, mother of Mr. Jo. Nicholls, keeper
of Ludgate.

8. Sir Hen. Slingsby and Dr. Hewitt, beheaded on
Tower Hill

July   7. Coll. Ashton } hanged, drawn, and quartered, in Tower
          & } Street and Cheapside, for there loyalty.
one Batteley }

Aug.   6. The Lady Claypole, the Protector's daughter, died at
Hampton Court.

8. Old Oliver Markland, once innkeeper at the Castle in
Wood Street, died at Stratford Bow.

14. The wife of Mr. Chard, sometime ye city smith, sister
to Mr. Lewes Bromhall, attorn. died at White Chappell, removed from Lothbury.

6. Mr. Robt. Dawkes, innkeeper at ye White Hinde in
Coleman Street, a constant appearer on juries,
buried.

20. Rich. Chambers, once alderman and sherriff of London,
died at Hornsey; buried ye 26.

Sept.   2. Sherriff Chandler died; Rich. Ring chosen sherriff to supply his place; buried 16.

3. Oliver, Lord Protector, died at Whitehall, his son Richard deputed Protector in his roome; his funeral. Nov. 9.

2. Mr. Waters, a cheesemonger by Christ Church, goeing well to bed at his inn at Stony Stratford, was found stark dead next morning.

7. Old Mis Floree, Mis Ladore's mother, died; buried 9.

8. Old Mr. Molyns, pewterer in Lothbury, died.

12. Mr. Bigg, attorn. in Ironmonger Lane, died.

6. Fran. Allen, alderman, died in the country; buried wth his wife Oct. 13, both at Lambeth.

16. Mounsier St. Giles, died.

Rich. Smith, once a vintner in Smithfield, died about this time.

John Redwood of the Crown Office died about this time.

9. Mr. Crook, once under sheriff, Midd. died.

28. Old Mr. Vaughan, of ye Remembr. Office in ye Exchequer, died.

29. Mr. Coleman, once dwelling in Bell Alley, in Coleman Street, died at Westminster.

28. Mis Read, at the Bell at Finsbury, died; and buried Octr. 2.

29. Mr. Ralph Hutchinson, vintner in Aldersgate Street, died.

8. Edw. Blackmore, stationer in St. Paul's Church Yard, died.

Octob.   7. Mr. Tho. Brooker, who married Sir Tho. Hamond's daughter, died.

9. Mr. Farringdon, preacher in Milk Street, died in the country, a famous preacher.

23. Coll. Tho. Pride (at first a drayman) died; his funerall at Nonsuch, Novem. 2.

30. Mr. Austin of Hogsden, ye elder brother, died.

31. Mr. Dorrington of King's Langley died.

31. Mr. Taylor, once an attorn. of the Court of Wards, died in London.

Novem.   4. Mr. Legat in Little Wood Street, printer, once printer at Cambridge, since distempered in his senses, died.

11. Charles Wheatley, son in law to Peter Herbert, died.

27. Jo. Powell of the Chamberlain's Office died of a consumption.

Rog. Norton, printer, who married Nell Houlker, died very poore.

Decem. 10. Mr. Peter Ladore, our loving neighbor, died.

11. Peregrin Herbert, clerk of ye Compter and an attorney, died in Wood Street; buried 14.

13. Dr. Matth. Brookes died in Criplegate parish; buried· ye 17 at St. Michaells in Whittington Colledg.

16. Alderman Pack's wife buried.

16. Mr. Grafton, upholster in Cornhill, buried.

16. Mr. Snow, baker in Bassinghall Street, died; buried 18.

19. Mr. Comber, of St. Giles, Criplegate, died; buried 22.

24. James Martyn, apothecary in Old Baily, died.

24. Mr. Andr. Price, sea surgeon, who married my coz. Dorothy, daughter to my brother Walter, died in Alborow Bay, in Suffolk. She after married Mr. . . . Calcott, attorn. of ye King's Bench Court.

30. Mr. Cowes, a warder of the Tower, buried, leaving a very good report behind him.

Januar.   7. Mr. Ralph Flower, father of Mr. Flower preacher in Lothbury, died at Kingston, and buried here in London.

Mr. Brisco, upholster in Old Jury, died.

13. Tho. White, once a bookseller wthout Algate, having left his trade, died in ye Old Jury, a very poore man.

15. Ralph, son of Mr. Aug. Newbold, died.

22. Rich. Myn, bookseller in Little Brittain, died; buried 25.

25. Mis Brand, daughter to Mr. Rogers, attorney at Kingston, wife to Mr. Brand hosier in Barbican, buried.

Febr. 22. Mr. Tho. Bowyer, merch^t in Old Jury, buried.

Mar. 3. Mr. Gideon de Lawne, apothecary in Black Friers, aged 92 years, buried.

17. Lislebone Long, Recorder of London, and Speaker of the Parliament, died.

22. Justice Lisle, at Saffron Hill, died; once a wollen draper in Cannon Street.

1659.

29. Rich. Brawn, eldest son of Sir Richard Brawn of King's Langley, died of the small pox; buried on Good Friday at Lanley.

April 7. Mr. Lawrence, brewer in Old Street, his funerall.

14. Mr. Warren, printer, died.

22. Peter Bourn, only sonn and child of Tho. Bourn, bookseller in Bedlam,ᵃ died, and buried the 26th.

May. 5. Barnard Pollard, bookseller, chiefly for romances and pamphletts in English, died.

6. My cozen Anne, daughter of my brother Walter Smith, died.

13. Rich. Dyke, keeper of Newgate, died.

13. Dean Fuller, vicar of Criplegate parish, died.

19. Old Mr. Tickner, grocer in Barbican, died; buried ye 26.

12. Chr. Hatton. once an attorn. in ye Excheq^r, buried in Northamptonshire.

26. Rob. Smith, inkeeper at ye Anchor in Litt. Britt.

June 9. Mr. Tho. Sallowes, grocer in Wood Street, buried at Redriff.

ᵃ In the street now called Liverpool Street, but then designated Bedlam Street, and subsequently Old Bedlam, the street leading to the site of the antient Hospital. See another entry in p. 53, and again p. 56.—ED.

Hum. Mitchell, sometime pewterer in Wood Street, and also his wife Grace, died about this time at Baldock.

23. Mr. Latham, councellor, died.

July 26. Ralph Brisco, clerk of Newgate, and} died.
Mary Frith, *als.* Mall Cut-purse,[a]

Ellis Young, attorn. Excheq^r, died about ye same time,

Aug. 28. Tho. Fludd, clerk of Cordweyners' Hall, died, and young Mr. Wm. Newbold succeeded him.

Sept. 29. Tho. Morton, Bp. of Durham, buried.

29. Barnes, glasier in Red Cross Street, died.

Octob. 7. Lambert Osbaldston, once schoolmaster at Westminster, buried.

10. Mr. Hynd, Remembrancer of London, died.

27. Mr. Ralph Collins, apothecary in Lothbury, buried.

31. Mr. Jo. Bradshaw, judge of ye Sheriff's Court in Guildhall, who pronounced sentence of death upon his soveraign, died; afterwards rediged and his head sett upon a poll over Westmin^r as a traitor.

Novem. 1. Mr. John Greene, Recorder of London, son to Sergeant Greene, died.

Ferd. Carby John, ye Portugall Jew, cutt of ye stone, died about this time.

11. Old Mis Rudd (once living in ye Poultry) died.

11. Mis Moyer, the stone cutter's wife in Little Brittan, died.

29. Mis Greene, wife to Mr. Greene, late Recorder, died in child bed; her child died ye day before.

Decem. 15. Mr. Wm. Harlow, merchant, my brother Walter's brother in law by his wife, died at Waltham Stow.

17. Bp. Brownrigg interred.

16. Walter Westcot, once a clerk of the Compter in Wood Street, buried.

Januar. 9. Dr. Lennard, phisician, died.

[a] See Granger, vol. ii. p. 407, for her character.

Februa. 8. Sam. Ward, sergeant of Wood Street, died.

March 1. Mr. Austin, of Hogsdon, ye yonger brother, died.

1660.

April 6. Nich. Brown, bookseller by ye Exchange, died.

6. Tho. Vnderhill, bookseller by Paul's Church, died.

7. Dr. Hen. Hammond died in Worcestershire.

21. Giles Edney, my wives brother, died a prisner in ye King's Bench; buried ye 23.

30. Mr. Walley, once clerk of Stationers' Hall, died in ye country.

August 10. Scott, a yeoman of ye Poultry Compter, died.

10. Mr. Hamond L'Estrange died in ye country.

30. Mr. Eastwood, at ye Last wthout Aldersgate, buried.

Septem. 13. Hen. Duke of Gloucester died of ye small pox.

20. Sir Rich. Stone, secondary of Wood Street, died.

21. Mis Dun, wife of Mr. Dun, and only child of Mr. Jerman, citty carpenter, died.

30. Mr. Chr. Muschamp died at Dr. Abbot's house in Shorditch, near the church.

Octob. 1. Mr. Wm. Manby, clerk of the Leather Sellers, buried.

12. Coll. Tho. Harrison (once my brother Houlker's clerk), hanged, drawn, and quartered for treason.

16. Cook & Hugh Peters executed at Charing Cross.

17. Scot, Clement, Jones, and Scroop executed.

17. Carew executed at ye same place.

Novem. 1. Old Ned Nicholls, attorn. died of an apoplexie.

27. John Lord Finch, once Lord Chief Justice of ye Comon Pleas, after Lord Keeper, a proud and impious man, but loyall to his prince.

Decem. 1. Mr. Johnson, preacher at Bassinghall, died.

18. Hen. Seile, bookseller in Fleet Street, died.

Mis Turnpenny, once wife to Mr. Kellam Smith, a ser-

geant of Wood Street, died at Litchfield about this
time.

24. The Lady Mary, Princess of Orange, and sister to K.
Charles 2d, died of yᵉ small pox.

Janua. 5. Tho. White, virginal maker in Old Jury, buried.

25. Tho. Smith, scrivener in Cornhill, son of Kellam Smith,
died.

Jan. 31. Hump. Mosely, bookseller in Paul's church yard, died;
buried Feb. 4.

Febr. 5. Mr. Lofeild, silkman in Lombard Street, buried at Islington.

17. Mⁱˢ Juice, wife of Mr. Juice, minister at King's Lanley, died.

15. Mr. Tatt paid me 50*s.* for a legacy (given me, my wife,
and daughter Houlker) by Mⁱˢ Ellyn Collyns deceased.

March 4. Mr. Matth. Awborn, Under Sherriff of Surry, died at
Kingston Assizes sodenly.

15. Egmondisham Pickays junior buried.

1661.

May. Mr. Horton, of Hogsdon, about this time died.

8. Old Mⁱˢ Anne Hutchison, wife to Mr. Hen. Hutchison in Poultry, died at her chamber in Bedlam
Street.

9. Mr. Dan. Waldo, of Cheapside, buried.

July 7. Mr. Franck, a juryman in Pilkington Court in Little
Brittain, died at Oxford.

11. Mr. John Rothwell, bookseller in Cheapside, died.

12. Ben. Wallinger, of the Pipe Office in Gray's Inn,
attorn. for the sheriffs of London, died about this
time.

21. Lionel Child, clerk-sitter in Wood Street, died.

Aug. 6. Sir Marm. Langdale died about this time.

8. Young Mr. Francklyn, son to Mr. Francklyn warder
at the Tower, died.

11. Sam. Cartwright, son of Sam. Cartwright bookseller
in Duck Lane, died.

14. Dr. Nicholas, Dean of St. Paul's, died.

16. Dr. Tho. Fuller, of the Savoy, died; buried at Gan-
ford* in Midd. by the Lord Barckly his patron there.
Dr. Hardy, Deane of Rochester, preached his funerall sermon.

16. Mr. Adams in St. Laurence Lane, who fined for alderman, died.

16. Mis Mosse, late wife of Mr. Clement Mosse, under
chamberlain, buried.

16. Old Mis Samon died.

17. Ant. Maria Smith, herald painter in Fleet Street, buried.

21. Mr. Cowper, minister of Shadwell, buried.

Septem.   5. Mr. Wm. Burroughs (my landlord), buried.

5. Lady Wild, wife of Sir Wm. Wild, recorder, buried.

5. Mr. Moyer, stone cutter in Little Britain, buried.

19. Mr. Paine of St. Giles, Criplegate, buried.

27. Mr. Tho. Smith, library keeper of Cambridge, died.

Octob.   1. Ephraim Andrews, merch^t, died about this time.

3. Mr. Tho. Burnell, merch^t in Coleman Street, buried.

6. Alderman Abraham Reynardson buried.

Novem.   16. Mr. Wm. Haselfoot, clerk of Goldsmiths' Hall, died,
and buried ye 19th.

29. Dr. Brian Walton, Bp. of Chester, died; buried
Decem. 4.

Decem.   5. Mr. Samuel Clarkson, of ye six Clerks Office, died.

6. Mr. Wm. Hambleton, a Scotish man, died a rigid
presbyterian.

10. Mr. Robert Robinson, once a clerk sitter of Wood
Street Compter, buried in St. Giles, Criplegate.

* Cranford.—ED.

17. Isaac Penington, late alderman, prisoner in yᵉ Tower, convict of high treason, died.

25. Owen Row, prisoner in yᵉ Tower for yᵉ same, died.

Febru. 12. Lady Elizabeth, relict to yᵉ Palsgrave, Queen of Bohemia, died here at Westminster.

Mar. 16. Mⁱˢ Littlebury, yᵉ first wife to Mr. Robt. Littlebury, bookseller in Little Brittain, died; buried 20.

17. Sir James Drax's funerall from Cambden House.

20. Alderman Chard (sometime city smith) buried.

1662.

March 25. Old Hen. Grant, in Birchin Lane, an Old Jury man, buried.

April 1. Mr. Harvey, vintner at the Starr in Coleman Street, died.

1. Mr. Roger Norton, printer in Black ffriers, died, whose daughter my coz. Dr. Tho. Cluterbuck marrᵈ.

2. Mr. Sam. Smith, preacher in Essex, buried.

7. Mr. Luke Cropley, died, a rich citizen.

13. Dr. Wm. Hall, of St. Michael Bassisshaw, died hydropticall.

19. Baxter, late Lieutᵗ of yᵉ Tower, Corbett, and Okey, traitors convict, executed at Tyborn.

22. Alderman Fowkes died of an apoplexy.

May 2. My sister Martha Houlker (our constant loving friend) died at Langley, there buried May 6.

2. John Hatr, brewer wᵗʰ out Criplegate, died; buried May 6.

8. Dr. Peter Heylyn, prebend at Westminster (a stirring man), a good schollar, died at Westminster on Ascention day.

13. Tho. Allen, parish clerk in Old Jury, died blind.

22. A woman burnt in Smithfield for killing her husband.

20. Sir Robt. Pye died at Westminster.

14. Sir Hen. Vane, (convict of high treason,) beheaded on
　　Tower Hill.

18. Mr. Griffith of Gray's Inn, my acquaintance, a good
　　scollar, died, being well ye day before; diverse
　　small books of his I bought of Mr. Fr. Myn at Mr.
　　Marshall's.

24. The old Porter next door to our house buried, whose
　　wife, for killing her infant, was formerly hanged.

27. Mr. Edw. Fetherston, attorn. of ye King's Bench, died;
　　buried June 30.

August 12. Mis Corney, lodging with Mis Kingston her kinswoman,
　　died; a woman of a loving disposition.

20. Mr. Laurence Brinley, in Aldermanbury, died.

23. Mr. Simon Ashe, preacher at St. Austin's in Watling
　　Street, buried.

26. Mis Godlington, of Hagerston, died.

Septem. 15. Dr. Brock, a physitian, about this time died.

19. Dr. John Gauden, Bp. of Worcester, late of Exeter,
　　died.

20. Mr. Biddle (the Socinian) died.

21. Mr. Sheires, bookseller in Covent Garden, buried.

Octob. 20. Mr. Walwyn, junior, a bricklayer in Criplegate parish,
　　died.

22. Capt. Tasker's only son and child buried.

Novem. 5. Mr. Wm. Liptrot, (once a scrivener,) who married my
　　daughter Smith's aunt, sister to her mother, died poore.

7. Tho. Robinson, vintner in Cheapside, died.

15. Mr. Hugh Audley, (sometime of ye Court of Wards,)
　　died infinitely rich.[a]

---

[a] The title of a Pamphlet published at this time may be worth adding. "The Way to
be rich, according to the practice of the Great Audley, who begun with *two hundred* pound,
in the year 1605, and dyed worth *four hundred thousand* pound this instant November
1662. *Rem quocunque modo Rem.*" 4to. Lond. 1662. Audley's christian name does
not appear throughout this pamphlet. —ED.

30. Capt. Greenhill, of Bedlam, cordweyner, buried at St. Ellens.

Decem. 10. Mr. Wm. Gunthorp, once sword-bearer to y⁰ Lord Mayor, died in Morefields.

18. Mr. John Thomas, apothecary in Wood Street, buried.

25. Mr. Stannard, scrivener wᵗʰout Aldersgate, died.

27. Mr. De Lawn, a merchᵗ in Lothbury, wᵗʰ his wife, whole family, and some lodgers, burnt wᵗʰ his house; not one person saved.

January 2. Mr. Ralph Hartley, apothecary in yᵉ Old Jury, a right honest man, and of a good estate.

6. Geo. Lord Goring, in his passage by land from Hampton Court to London, died at Brentford, aged about 80.

9. Mr. John Squier, reader of Barnes in Surrey, only son of John Squier, minister once of Shorditch, died.

20. The little blackmore boy at Mⁱˢ Ladore's buried.

29. Mr. Porter, a rich man in Great St. Bartholm. died.

Februa. 27. Mⁱˢ Rose Flewellen, wife to Mr. Wm. Flewellen, keeper of Guildhall, buried in Lothbury Church.

March 5. Mr. Wm. Badger, gardner in Shorditch, aged near 100 years (who died yᵉ last Febr.) now buried.

19. Mⁱˢ Franklyn, in Ropemakers Alley, died; a woman very free of her tongue.

ᴸ 1663.

April 12. Mr. Merrick, a merchᵗ in Criplegate parish, died where he had not long time dwelt.

16. Old Mⁱˢ Bateman, yᵉ relict of Mr. Robert Bateman, once Chamberlain of London; buried in St. Dunstans in yᵉ east.

17. Old Nan Wilmot in Little Brittain died.

22. Mr. Tho. Robinson, bookseller at Oxford, died wᵗʰ a good report of an honest man.

May　　　10. Mr. Francklyn of Ropemakers Alley, a poore man,
　　　　　　　died in yᵉ hospitall in Southwark.

June　　　4. Dr. John Juxon, A.Bp. Canterbury, removed from
　　　　　　　London, died at Lambeth, with a good report for his
　　　　　　　loyalty to King Charles yᵉ Martyr.

　　　　　　4. Old Mr. John Bunbury, clerk of Grocers' Hall, died.

　　　　　　6. Ralph Rounthwait, stationer, buried at St. Faith's.

　　　　　14. Mr. Tho. Whatman, our next neighbor, died; buried
　　　　　　　in Bassinghall Church 18th.

　　　　　13. The Countess of Bridgwater going to the Earl, her
　　　　　　　husband, then a prisoner under the Black Rod,
　　　　　　　committed by the Parliament wᵗʰ the Earl of Midd.
　　　　　　　to yᵉ Tower, died at yᵉ Black Rod's house in child bed.

　　　　　26. Mr. John Allen, of Graies Inn, one of yᵉ city Councell,
　　　　　　　died at Graies Inn this day.

July　　　1. Mr. Basile, at Hampton Court, died.

　　　　　　6. Mr. Fox, steward of St. Barthol. Hospitall, buried.

　　　　　22. Hen. Lucas, Esqʳ, a learned and judicious gentleman,
　　　　　　　buried at the Temple, dying at his lodgins in Chancery
　　　　　　　Lane, a batchellor; he bequeathed his choice library
　　　　　　　of books to . . . . Colledg, in Cambridge.[a]
　　　　　　　Dr. Heywood, Rector of St. Giles in yᵉ Fields, died.

August.　　Sim. Burton, an oyleman wᵗʰ out Algate, sometime
　　　　　　　prentice to Mr. Aspley, bookseller, died.

　　　　　11. Old Mr. Marre, in Little Morefields, buried.

　　　　　21. Mr. Newborn, solliciter in Old Jury, died.

Septem.　15. Stephen Fawcet, surgeon in Wood Street, died wᵗʰ a
　　　　　　　good name of an honest and pious man, who in his
　　　　　　　time sett up a lecture in St. Giles parish wᵗʰ out

---

[a] Henry Lucas, Esq. was the founder of the Lucasian professorship at Cambridge.
His books were not bequeathed to any College, but to the Library of the University, "to
supply as far as he could the loss occasioned by the removal of the Lambeth Library."
See the Preface to Dr. Barrow's Mathematical Lectures, and Ackerman's History of the
University of Cambridge, vol. ii. p. 142.—ED.

Criplegate, for every week in Lent, a sermon for
ever.

Octob.   4. Sir Robt. Forster, Lord Ch. Justice of ye King's
Bench, died at Windsor.

Octob.   30. Mr. Norwood, of Stanmore, who married ye eldest
daughter of Mr. Cornel. Bee, bookseller, died of a
feavor.

Novem.   6. Rand. Manwaring's funerall at Edmonton.

14. Mr. Baxter, apothecary in Coleman Street, died of a
pleurisy, lately before married.

11. Sir Robt. Wood, of Islington, buried at Clerkenwell.

20. Mr. Sale, of Lymehouse, son of Capt. Sale, ye last
husband of my sister Parker, of the Bermudas, died.
Old Proudlove, bellman of Criplegate, buried.

Decem.   Mr. Arnold, a linnen weaver and maker of mouth glue,
died about this time.

4. Old Mr. Tho. Smith, our neighbor at ye corner house
in Little Morefields, in ye Lordsh. of Finsbury, died.

6. Judge Jenkins, aged 81 years, died in Wales.

19. Mis Herbert, late wife of Mr. Peregrin Herbert, of
Stanwell, clerk-sitter of Wood Street Compter, buried
at Michaell's, Wood Street.

16. Mis Clerk, wife to Mr. Clerk, minis^r at St. Ethel-
burgh, died in London, and buried at Tottenham 22.

Janua^r.   1. Mr. Nottingham, our brewer's clerk, buried at Criplegate.

21. James Turnor, a sollicitor, comonly call Coll. Turnor,
hanged at Lyme Street end, for robbing Mr. Fr.
Fryon, mercht.

23. Mr. Guyet, of Hagerston, buried.

Febru.   2. Mr. Augar, sometime school m^r at Mercers Chapel,
buried.

22. Mr. Ewen, sometime clerk of ye Lord Mayor's Court,
died sodenly.

Nath. Butter, an old stationer, died very poore.

28. M^ls Mary De New, late wife of Mr. Peter La Dore, died in childbed of her first and only child by Mr. De New, her last husband.

March 10. Jam. De New, ye only child of Mr. De New, by his wife lately deceased, buried.

1664.

April At the later end of this month died, and was buried at Putney, Mr. Wm. Wymonsold, of the Exchequer, of ye Treasurer Remembrancer's Office.

May 13. Sir Tho. Widrington, sergeant at law, died.

25. My dear wife *(hei mihi)* M^ls Elizabeth Smith died this dismall night; buried ye 28 of May.

29. My old friend and quondam fellow, Mr. Wm. Newbold, in the Old Jury, attorn. died; buried June 2.

June 3. My coz. Wyn, sister to Mr. Tho. Dayrell, buried.

July 11. The fatt Porter at ye Axe in Aldermanbury buried.

22. M^ls Webb, in White Cross Street, mother to Mr. Webb, our late reader in St. Giles Criplegate, died.

22. Mr. Pepper, a mealeman at the Cundict w^thout Criplegate, buried.

30. Mr. Chantrell, needle-maker ag^st St. Giles Church, buried.

Augt. 2. Mr. Laur. Sadler, bookseller, died at ye Hague of ye plague.

12. Mr. Jo. Whithorn, chandler in Aldersgate Street, died.

22. Mr. Bosuile, a wollen draper w^thout Ludgate (my debtor), buried.

A son, an infant of Coz. Harby, srivener, husband to Mari Houlker, buried. She since was married to one Statham.

Septem. 1. Mr. Brigs, in Redcross Street (my pew fellow), died in ye country.

Septem. 2. Laur. Blomley, clerk of Cooks Hall, and alderman's deputy of Aldersgate w^{th}out, died of an apoplex.

3. Dan. Pakeman, bookseller in Fleet Street, buried.

12. Jo. Sadler, son to Laur. Sadler, bookseller in Little Brittain, died.

17. Mr. Gilbert Barrell, of Clifford's Inn, buried at Aleworth.

17. M^{ls} Torey, a sattin cap maker in Morefields, died.

22. M^{ls} Thomas, ye relict of Mr. Thomas, apothecary in Great Wood Street, died this morning.

30. Mr. White, late attorn. of the Mayor's Court (haveing lately sold his place), being very well at 5 of ye clock in the evening died at 8 y^t night.

Octob. 3. Mr. Throgmorton Trotman, merchant in Little Morefields, uncle to Secondary Trotman, died.

9. Old Mr. Thom. Godfrey died in Kent.

22. Dr. John Barwick, Dean of St. Paul's, died; buried 27. Anthony Burgess, once preacher at St. Laurence Jury, about this time died.

27. M^{ls} Prockson, wife to Mr. Procson, minister at St. Stephens, of Coleman Street, and daughter to Mr. Gilbert, a nonconformist, died.

29. Mr. Meredith, our neighbor in Little Morefields, died at Cambery* by Islington; buried in Criplegate parish Nov. 3.

30. M^{ls} Brigs grandchild, in Redcross Street, died of ye small pox.

Novem. 13. Mr. Miles Flesher, printer, died this morning, being well at 7 of ye clock; buried at Butolph's, Aldersgate, Novem. 17.

16. M^{ls} Abbot, once wife to Mr. Hanson, of Whitington Colledge, and before to Mr. Clutterbuck, died.

---

* Canonbury.—ED.

20. Mr. James Windet died at his house in Milk Street; buried there ye 24 ; Dr. Outram preached.

Decem.   7. Mis Ward, widdow, once wife of Mr. Staples, buried in St. Giles Criplegate, where is her husband Staples monument.

8. Mis Anne Newbold, wife of Mr. Aug. Newbold, Old Jury, buried.

9. My cozen Fran. Smith, daughter to my brother Walter.

9. Mr. James Denew, our neighbor in Morefields, died; buried in St. Giles Criplegate, Dec. 14, wth rings.

15. Our neighbor, Mr. Ward's kinswoman and servt. killed with ye fall of a chimney in ye Postern, as she passed by; buried ye 17.

24. Mr. Rich. Satterthwait, scrivener in Wood Street, died; buried 31.

Janu.   17. Little Tom Fleetwood, my son Fleetwood's child, died.

24. Mr. Meering, late an officer in Wood Street, died.

28. Dr. D. Trigg, *Empericus famosus*, died; bur^d Feb. 3.

Febru.   1. Deputy Antrobus, wollen draper in St. Paul's Church Yard, died.

6. Tho. Wild, attorney, brother to Sir Wm. Wild, Recorder, buried.

11. Old Mis Pitts, wife to Edw. Pitts, at Balms, died, aged (upon report) 105 years.

1665.

March   26. Nathan Webb, bookseller in Paul's Church Yard, died; buried ye 31.

29. Mr. Read Salter, in Lad Lane, died.

April   11. Fran. Ladore, son of Mr. Peter Ladore, in More Fields, died; buried Apr. 13.

15. A daughter of Mr. Hamson, in Grub-street, aged about 18 years, died.

18. My son, Jeffrey Fleetwood, died in ye Tower, leaving my daughter Anne, his wife, and 6 small children behind him. God prosper them.

May

3. My old coz. Katherin Bitcliff, died at her house at Lymes End in Buckinghamshire.

5. Mr. Stanton, in Shoe Lane, uncle to my late maid, Anne Vize, died.

23. Cosen Geo. Owen (late Herald) died in Pembrokeshire, leaving behind him my cosen Rebecca his relict, ye only daughter of Sir Tho. Dayrell, of Lyllingston, living.

This month died Mr. Billing, in Little Morefields, once a bayliff of Middx.

This night died my old acquaintance Mr. Nicholas Herrick, in Goodman's Fields.

June

1. Sir Tho. Vyner, goldsmith (once Ld Mayor), his funerall from Goldsmiths' Hall.

6. Mr. Adam Smith, our neighbor, this Tuesday died, lying a little while, about 2 or 3 days, sick.

10. Mr. Holland, apothecary in Great Wood Street, died, wth a good name of an honest man.

21. Mr. Andrews, w^{th}out Criplegate, died; buried ye 27 at St. Mart. Orgars.

25. General Lawson, died at Greenwich of his wounds in the last sea fight with the Dutch.

July

4. My cos. Eliz. Houlker, died of ye plague at her sister Harbyes house in White Cross Street.

5. Ferdinando Sothern, sexton of Criplegate parish, died, having not lyen sick above a day or two, and so suspected to have died of ye sickness, but not retorned.

3. Alexander Davis, scrivener, died at Westminster, suspected (not retorned) of the plague; his mother, Mis Davis, in Old Jury, died there.

16. Cosen Harby's young child died in his house infected, and the nurse keeper in the same house, of y° plague.

21. Mr. Pechell, preacher, son in law to Mr. Musgrave, plaisterer in Aldermanbury, died, and buried, *ex peste.*

Mr. Jackson, head keeper of Newgate, died this month *ex peste.*

M. Daykyn, bookseller, a recusant, in High Holborn, died there *ex peste.*

Aug^st. 1. Mr. Wm. Procter, vintner at y° Mitre in Wood Street, wth his young son, died at Islington (insolvent) *ex peste.*

8. M^ls Dorothy Muschamp, daughter to M^ls Muschamp, M^ls Harlow's sister, died in Old Street *ex peste,* her brother dying a little before *ex peste.*

9. Old Mr. Reading, of Criplegate parish, died *ex peste.*

9. Wm. Harby, scrivener in White Cross Street, died of y° plague, who married Mary Houlker, who was since married to Mr. . . . . . Statham.

9. Mr. Lightfoot, in Great More Fields, y° City painter, *ex peste.*

9. Capt. Downes, Capt. to Lieut. Tho. Fleetwood, died at Islington *ex peste.*

John Jones, bookseller in Little Brittain, died about this time of a consumption, in the country.

10. Nell, sometime M^ls Harlow's maid, died at M^ls Muschamp, in Old Street, *ex peste.*

10. Our late maid, Nell Hutchins' sister, died at y° Pest House *ex peste.*

10. Old M^ls Langham, M^ls Muschamp's landlady, died.

12. M^ls Bliseard, in Beech Lane, one of our churchwardens of Criplegate, buried *ex peste.*

12. Mr. Winckle, a chandler in Little Morefields, died.

12. Dr. Abbott, late of Shoreditch, died *ex peste.*

Aug. 14. Nell our late maid's father in law, married to her mother, died in Tenter Alley in Morefields, died *ex peste*.

20. Nell, our maid's mother, in Tenter Alley, newly married, died ther *ex peste*.

Mr. Player, in Tower Street, goldsmith, died of a consumption.

20. Mis Pyne, wife of Mr. Pyne, our parish clerke, of St. Giles Criplegate, died *ex peste*.

21. Mis Withers, wife to our neighbor, Mr. Withers, in Little Moreffields, died.

16. Mr. Peachy, in Bishop's gate street, who lately married Mis Baker, daughter to Mr. Whatmore, died a week or more since *ex peste*.

22. Mis Wincle, Mr. Wincle's wife, ye chandler, who died ye 12 past, died *ex peste*.

Mr. Winckfield, ye school Mis husband in Angell Alley, died.

22. Wm. Musgrave, plaisterer in Aldermanbury, died; buried 23.

26. Mis Alice Barker, wife to Mr. Matth. Barker, attor. in Wood Street, died *plena dierum et bonæ famæ;* buried ye 30.

26. Mr. Robt. Yarrow, scrivener in Woodstreet, died at his country house *ex peste*.

27. Mr. James Acton, attorn. Comon Pleas, died in Aldersgate Street; buried Aug. 30th; *ex peste*.

28. Paul White, cook in Little Brittain, buried; died *ex peste*.

August. Wm. Guyett (old goodwife Wenham's husband), near ye Jamaica in Shoreditch, died *ex peste*, wth his little boy.

Dr. Burnet, in Fenchurch Street, physitian, died about this time *ex peste*.

Aug.   Mis Tredway, wife of Mr. Tredway at Hagerston, about this time died *ex peste.*

Mr. Brown, once a bookseller at ye Hague, who married ye daughter of Mr. Nath. Hall of ye Excheq^r, died at ye Pest house *ex peste,* about this time.

26. Mis Coare, wife to Rich. Coare, chandler in Lothbury, in Old Jury parish, died.

Sibb. old Mis Hutchinson's maid, about this time died.

About this time died Mis Haggen and her daughter Jane *ex peste.*

Septem. 1. Mr. Rott, blacksmith in Bedlam, died, and buried in Criplegate Church ; *ex peste.*

1. Mis Shirley, wife to Mr. John Shirley, bookseller in Little Brittain, buried.

1. Robt. Stone, broker in Barbican, buried.

2. Mary White, ye relict of Thom. White, virginall maker, my late tennant in Old Jury, buried, *ex peste.*

Glover, the smith at London Wall, and his wife (about this time both) died *ex peste.*

2. Nell Hutchins, our late servant, died in Tenter Alley, *ex peste.*

2. Mis Durant, of Criplegate parish, our pew fellow, buried in this parish ; *ex peste.*

2. Mr. Snow, gardner in Shoreditch parish, buried, *ex peste.*

Mr. Hyett, debtor to my late sonne Fleetwood, clerk of the Vintners' Company, died at Vintners' Hall *ex peste.*

5. Anne Mayhew, wife to Mr. Tho. Mayhew at London Stone, died at Mowsham Hall, by Chelmsford, Essex.

5. Mis Powell, wife to Mr. Powell bookbinder in Little Brittain, died ; buried ye 6th ; *ex peste.*

Septem. 6. Webster, ye old drunken cobler, under my tennant
Bennings stall in Coleman Street, buried at Annis
de Clere, at his owne desire; *ex peste.*

11. Mr. Wollaston, our neighbor in White's Alley, his 4th
child (at home), buried, all of ye plague.

10. Old goodwife Guyett (by Jamaica), having before
buried her husband and her little boy, buried at
Stepney also, all of ye plague.

9. Mr. Fox, husband to Mis Robinson in Silver Street,
cakewoman, buried, *ex peste.*

10. John Boston's wife, in an alley in Little Morefields,
buried, *ex peste.*

11. Tho. Cooper, journeyman bookseller to Mr. R. Royton,
died *ex peste.*

12. Mis Willett, cakewoman in Wood St. near Lad Lane,
died *ex peste.*

15. Mr. Edw. Ball, ironmonger in Poultry, died at Chelsey; buried ye 15 in the Poultry.

15. Old John Wharton, of Guildhall, buried; died of old
age.

16. Mr. Cherry, rope maker, our honest neighbor in Morefields, died this morning early *ex peste.*

18. Wm. Gore, escheator of London, died in Surrey.

15. Mr. Raworth, minister of Shorditch, died *ex peste.*

14. Mr. Long, preacher at St. Alphage, died *ex peste.*

14. Alderman Bide, at Hagerston, died *ex peste.*

15. Collyns, bookseller agst ye Church in Little Brittain, died
ex peste.

19. John Wharton, bricklayer, son of old John Wharton,
of ye Guildhall, buried, *ex peste.*

14. Thurloes son (our taylor), in Little Old Baily, died
ex peste.

22. Mr. Osbaldston, grocer, clerk of St. Butolphs Aldersgate, died *ex peste.*

Sept.   20. Mr. Hadman, of the same parish, died *ex peste.*

About this time Mis Ellis and her child by her former husband, Brown, coachman in White Cross Street, died *ex peste.*

21. Mr. Cutts, of St. Bartholomew's, buried.

22. Mis Dashwood, in Little Morefields, died *ex peste.*

20. Mr. Morton, Coroner of London, died *ex peste.*

21. Mr. Holden, at ye Red Cross in Little Brittain, died *ex peste.*

Dr. Bird (as commonly called), to whom I lent 20*s.* (a desperat debtor), died *ex peste.*

19. Mis Bennyns, wife of Tobias Bennyg, my tenant in Coleman Street, buried *ex peste.*

25. Geo. Dalton, Remembrancer (who ought my daught^r 50*l.*), died in St. Mary Axe *ex peste:* Capt. Burroughs succeeded.

24. Mr. Ward, shoemaker, brother to our neighbor Ward in Morefields, and 5 of his children, died *ex peste.*

27. Goodwife Hunt, the cobler's wife, sist^r to goodwife Jones ye milkwoman, buried.

29. Peter Stynt, in Pycorner, picture seller, died *ex peste.*

29. Simon Smith, in Seething Lane, an expert accomptant, died.

Octob^r.   1. John Scott, carpenter near ye Tower, died *ex peste.*

1. John Jones, son to Mis Jones lodging at our neighbor Mis Bradberd's, died *ex peste.*

Mis Jones, mother to John Jones, a lodger at Mis Bradberd's, died *ex peste.*

About this time died Jonings, our smith in Whitecross Street, *ex peste.*

7. Mis Flaxen, wife to Mr. Flaxen in White's Alley, my daughter Hacker's tenant, died *ex peste.*

7. Mr. Hobart, at Mis Cherrey's house, our neighbor (after his two daughters, who died before him), *ex peste.*

Octob^r. 6. Mis Myn, wife to Fran. Myn, bookseller in Little Brittain, and one of their children, died *ex peste.*

3. Mis Allen, ye little crooked woman once dwelt in Whites Alley, died.

10. The only daughter of Mr. Wells, in Gun Alley, buried, *ex peste;* 2 of his family died before, *ex peste.*

10. Joseph Cherry, younger son of our neighbor Mr. Cherry, rope maker, died *ex peste.*

13. Dr. Tho. Harrison, preacher at Christoph^rs, and before at St. Bartholomews, died *ex peste;* buried 14.

12. Fran. Myn, bookseller, in Little Brittain, son of Richard Myn, buried *ex peste.*

12. Old goodwife Veare, nurse to my brother Walter's family in London, removed thence, buried.

13. Mr. Hulcock, parish clerk of St. Mich. Basheshaw, buried, *ex peste.*

15. Mis Wright, wife to Mr. Wright, taylor in ye parish of Olaves Silver Strete, died *ex peste.*

15. Tho. Paybodie, a printer, buried, *ex peste.*

Mr. Wade, a baker in Whitecross Street, died this week, who had before buried his wife and servant; *ex peste.*

18. Pitt, vinegar man, who sold aples against Mr. Ladores house, died.

13. Mis Yarway, the scrivener's wife, died at Woodford Bridge *ex peste.*

23. Mr. Flaxen, our neighbour, my daughter Hackers tennant, died this night *ex peste.*

22. Mis Whatman dying at her daughter Peachyes house wth out Bishopsgate, buried; not of ye sickness.

20. John Tridway, of Hagerston, died *ex peste;* debtor to me 150*li.*, and 30*li.* to my daughter Hacker.

27. Mr. Knight in ye Postern, strongwater man, Lieut. of our traine band in ye Ward, died this night, *ex peste.*

*Octob*ʳ. 27. Mⁱˢ Neason, my sister Edney's sister, died *ex peste;* buried yᵉ 28, and her husband married again Nov. 5.

29. Mr. Everard, goldsmith in Lombard Street (who had fined for alderman), died *ex peste.*

Dr. Griffith, about this time (this month), died in the country; he was once pastor in St. Madal, Old Fish Street.

Novemb. 2. Mr. Royston, a young gentleman, a lodger at our neighbor Mⁱˢ Brabant, buried, *ex peste.*

3. Mr. Snelling's son, hat-band maker in Tenter Abbey, died *ex peste.*

10. Mr. Brackston, stockinseller in Forest street wᵗʰout Criplegate, buried, *ex peste.*

13. The Lady Blandina Foster, wife of Sir Regnald Forster, buried in Criplegate Church.

About this time died young Mr. Wakeman, minister of St. Matth. Fryday Street, *ex peste.*

About this time died Mr. Grove, plumer in Lad Lane, wᵗʰ his wife and whole family (except his partner), *ex peste.*

Decemb. 4. Peter Cole, bookseller and printer in Cornhill, hanged himselfe in his warehouse in Leadenhall; reported to be distracted.

4. Mⁱˢ Boot, comb-maker's widdow, next door to my brother Walter Smith's on Ludgate Hill, died.

9. Mⁱˢ Vancourt, wife of Peter Vancourt in Grub Street, on Thursday brought to bed, died this day; retorned this day seavennight out of yᵉ country in very good health, wᵗʰ her family in two coaches and four horses a piece.

11. John Smithier, once a scrivener (and attorn. Com. Pleas), landlord to Mr. Royston in Ireland, buried from the post house at . . . behind yᵉ Exchange.

Januar.   7. Rich. Draper, of ye Pettie Bagg Office, died at Finchley, my familiar friend.

      1. Mr. Blemell, minister of All Hallows ye Great in Thames Street (son of Thom. Blemell carpent^r in Old Jury), a good scholler, died at ye begining of this month.

    11. Ezech Trott, chander in Coleman Street, died.

    23. Mr. John Shirley, bookseller in Little Britain, *hora* 10 *sub nocte*, died.

    23. Old Mr. Bland at Twittenham died.

    20. Mr. Ford, grocer of Coleman Street, against London Wall, died *ex peste*.

Feb.   6. Mis Marshall, wife to Mr. John Marshall attorn. in Fetter Lane, buried Thursday, Feb. 8.

    21. My cozen Coleman's brother, a grocer at ye corner house in Coleman Street, next Beech Lane, blown up wth gunpowder, by a sparke of fire falling into a gunpowder barrell from a pipe of tobacco.

March   16. My loving and elder sister Mis Fran. Clutterbuck, widdow, died at her daughter Langston's house in Lincolnshire.

    20. Capt. Luke Fawne, bookseller at ye Parrott in Paul's Church Yard, died.

    17. Mis Martyn, wife to Tho. Martyn upholster in Cornhill, died.

1666.

Mr. Rich. Glyde, mercer, treasurer of Christ's Hospitall, died.

April   6. Greg. Markham, upholster, our neighbor in Little More fields, buried.

    10. Geo. Thomasin, bookseller, buried out of Station^{rs} Hall (a poore man).[a]

---

[a] This was George Thomason, who formed the singular Collection of Books, Tracts, and single Sheets, from 1640 to 1660, now preserved in the British Museum, and known by the name of "The King's Pamphlets." They were purchased and presented to the British Museum by His Majesty King Geo. III. in 1762.—ED.

April   16. Capt. Burroughs, muster master, clerk of the Company of Distillers, and the City Remembrancer, who succeeded Mr. Dalton late Remembranc^r, died poore.

          17. Tho. Cox, an oatemealeman in Shoe Lane, my sister Edney's acquaintance, died of a dropsie.

May   13. Old Tho. Fairclough, field keeper of Morefields, died; buried Tuesday May 15, having lived married 54 years wth his surviving wife.

          18. Mr. . . . . . Alexander, comon cryer of ye city, buried at his country house at Hadley by Barnett.

          21. Mis Rhodes, wife to Mr. Rhodes bookseller in Jewen Street near Criplegate, died.

          29. Mr. Vpton, m^r of the Pest House, buried (not of ye plague) in the middle isle of St. Giles church.

          31. Mis Winch, wife to Mr. Winch of the Chamberlain's office, died in ye country; an honest wife and good houswife.

June   3. Sir Francis Prujan, Kt. d^r of phisick, died (*plenus dierum, plenus numorum*).

          29. Alexander Broome, an attorn. King's Bench, an ingenious poet, died.

July   19. Old Mr. Boone, chirurgeon, buried.

August   7. Old Mr. Jackson, sometimes minister of St. Michael's Wood Street, there buried in ye ruines.

          7. Cooper, a barber in Aldersgate Street, buried in Botolph's parish there.

          11. Capt. Willis, at Haggerston, our acquaintance, buried.

          20. My cozen Rich. Clutterbuck fell sick and died in Leicestershire.

          22. Old Mr. Wells, in Gun Alley in Little Morefields, died; buried in ye new churchyard beyond ye Artillery Garden.

          31. Tho. Bolton, at the Bolt & Ton in Cornhill, buried.

Septem.   14. John Elsworth, a leather sock maker in Maiden Lane next Haberdashers' Hall, died.

Octob^r. 15. Wm. Lincoln, sometime my clerk in ye Poultry Compter, died at ye East Indies.

3. Lieu^t. Tho. Fleetwood, brother to my son Jeffry Fleetwood, being in the fleet at sea, returned to London sick of a burning feaver, and thereof died this day, of a mean estate, leaving behind a good report of an honest man.

6. Alderman Mennell, goldsmith, died.

19. Mr. John Myn, grocer w^thout Aldersgate, his son buried, who died on ye 15.

21. Mis Mynors, my sister Edney's cozen, wife to Mr. Mynors, beadle of the Drapers' Company, died in Beach Lane.

22. John Warner, Bp. of Rochester, died, *plenus dierum et numorum.*

Novem. 7. Edmond Calamy, once minister of St. Mary Aldermanbury, buried in ye ground of his late parish then demolished by ye fire; he was brought from Enfield.

Mr. Winstanly, of Grayes Inn, barrister, died this month.

Decem. 31. Mr. John Sawyer, of Batersey, died, once clerk of the papers at Wood Street.

Januar. 5. Old Mis Bunbury, relict of Mr. John Bunbury, attorn. Comm. Pleas, and clerk of Grocers' Hall, buried from Grocers' Hall ruines.

7. Honest William, once servant to Mis Ladore, and Mr. James Dellew our neighbour, died; buried Jan. 7.

4. Mr. Smith, linnen draper in Paul's Alley, a Recusant, died, being well the day before.

11. Mr. Francis Tryon, a rich merchant, buried.

23. Mr. Benson, bookseller in Chancery Lane, died.

25. Mr. Kniveton, clockmaker once in Lothbury, since the fire, in Bedlam, died.

Febru.   9. Mr. Major, mercer, husband to Mis Royston's daughter, died at Hackney; buried 14.

March   9. Nathan Nowell, bookseller in Little Brittain, died.

166⅞.   Old Sir Wm. Parkhurst, Kt. Master of the Mynt, buried at St. Peter ad Vincula in the Tower.

1667.

April   3. Mis Harvey, sister to Mr. Matth. Barker, attorn. once wife to Clement Harvey, brother to Sir Job Harvey, died this morning in Jewen Street near Criplegate; buried Apr. 5.

           4. Mr. Gardner, a warder at ye Tower, died.

          12. Mr. Barnes, who had fined for Alderman, buried.

          24. Dr. Matth. Wren, Bp. of Ely, died this night.

          16. Mr. Edw. Pitts, of Balmes by Hagerston, being in drink at Shacklewell, by a fall of his horse brake his skull, and died speachless.

May   11. About this time Tho. Hacker, servant to Mr. Hum. Robinson, bookseller, was unfortunately killed by the fall of a coach on him at shipboard at Flushing, being landing from England.

           7. Old Mr. Alderman Cleue, my brother Walter's great friend, died at Richmond, *plenus dierum et numorum.* He bequeathed many large legacies to Hospitalls and other pious uses, and 200*li.* to my broth^r Walter.

          25. Old Kelsey, the rich alehouse keeper at the Bear by Long Alley, Great Morefields, who married his daughter (a sober and religious virgin) unto Mr. Andrew Cater's son in Coleman Street, wth 1000*li.* portion at least.

          28. Old Bromley, a bodyes maker near Moor Lane, died sodenly; well and lusty ye day before.

             The Duke of Cambridge, eldest son of ye Duke of York, being dangerously sick, was about ye midst of

this month prayed for in all Churches, his younger
brother being lately before dead.

May 29. Mr. Eanth, vintner agst ye Spittle in Bishopsgate street,
died.

This week died John Hamond, a spruce taylor in St.
Martin's L' Grand, at his house at Romford.

Mr. George Withers, poet, died this month.

June 13. This night my old landlady, Mis Morris at Hagerston,
died; buried ye 13.

20. Duke of Cambridge, eldest son to ye Duke of Yorke,
died.

29. Sir Geo. Smith (a London merchant), a chief officer of
ye blew regiment, died this evening in Criplegate
parish, and there buried, wthout a sermon, July 4.

24. Mr. Tho. Hazard, a broker in Hounsditch, once a Sergeant at ye Poultry Compter, died.

26. My old cosen Peter Dayrell died at his house at Lillingston Dayrell, aged 82 years: his son Peter succeeded him in his estate at Lillingston, who died Feb.
20th, 1670.

July. Dr. Fairclough wife died this morning early after she
was newly delivered of a male child, living; she was
buried the next day at the parish church of St.
Giles in ye fields, wherein they dwelt.

11. Mr. Harrison's daughter, late in Grub Street, dying in
ye country, was this day buried in Criplegate church,
London. Dr. Parre of Camberwell, beneficed also
at St. Magdal. Bermundsey, in Southwark, preachd
her Funeral Sermon.

11. Holms, a notable thiefe and actor in setting of houses on
fire, being hanged, was buried in ye New Church
yard in the fields, in Criplegate parish.

9. The Lady Barkham, wife to Sir Edw. Barkham of
Tottenham, Kt. died.

26. Mr. Sproston, minister in Coleman Street, died this morning; buried at St. Alphage July 29.

Edm. Muschamp, late a prisoner in Aldgate for debt, died a poore man.

August   1. Sir Edw. Barkham died at his house at Tottenham.

Tho. Seaman, attorn. died July 31; buried Aug. 2 in St. Mildred Poultry's ruines.

8. Mills, the ensigne of ye Auxiliares, an alehouse keep^r in Little Morefields, died.

7. Jonas Proest, late preacher at ye Dutch Church, once dwelling in Morefields; being struck wth a dead palsie continued speechless till Wednesday the 17th after, and then died, and was buried in ye Dutch Church on Monday Aug. 12 wth a sermon in Dutch.

9. Mis Muschamp, widdow to Mr. Edw. Muschamp lately deceased, and sister to Mis Harlow and my brother Walter's wife, died this day, abought a fortnight after her husband, a woman of good report, sober, discreet, and good conditioned.

13. Dr. Jeremy Taylor, Bp. of Down in Ireland, much lamented and much wanted, died.

Septem. 21. Greg. Hardwick, clerk of Middleton's Water Works, once a vintner at ye Paul Head at Paul's chaine; buried in St. Gregories by Paul's.

20. Wm. Medlicot, a salter, sometime living in Cateaton Street by Guildhall, died.

Octob.   This month Joseph Kirton, sometime a bookseller at ye King's Arms in Paul's Church Yard, died; buried in St. Faith's.

2. The Lord of Colrane died sodenly at his house at Totteridge.*

---

* Hugh Lord Coleraine. He was buried at Totteridge, Oct. 9.—ED.

5. Roger Daniell, paynter in London, and sometime
heretofore at Cambridge, died in Lond.; buried from
his son in law Redman's house at St. Gregories.

Novem. 22. Old Nott, the taylor, once living in ye Old Jury, aged
about 100 years, died in Criplegate parish.

20. Weaver, at ye Arrowe in Finsbury, buried.

Decem. 29. Edw. Croft, bookseller against St. Buttolph's Church
in Little Brittain, died *hora* 5ta *ante merid.*; his relict,
remarried since to Mr. Blagrave, an honest book-
seller, who live hapily in her house in Little Brittain.

Januar. 7. Hannah Marriott, daughter of Mr. Marriott in Little
Morefields, buried.

Febru. 9. Old Mr. Yates, refyner of Criplegate parish, a constant
churchman, died.

9. Mr. Wm. Oglethorp, attorn. King's Bench Court, died
in Southwark (about this time).

26. Mis Alestry, wife to Mr. James Allestry, booksell^r,
buried in Little St. Bartholomew's, near Smithfield;
who died Feb. 22; Dr. Stillingfleet preached y^e
sermon.

24. Old Sir Tho. Adams, alderman of London, died.

27. Gabr. Bedell, bookseller wthin Temple Barr, died (by
taking a cup of poyson, as is reported).

21. John Thurloe, sometime Secretary of State, died.

March 2. Mr. Clynton's wife, silk dyer in Coleman Street, died.
166⅞. About this time died Tho. West, a cryer of ye Common Pleas, aged near 100 years.

1668.

April 19. Dr. Geo. Bates, a learned physitian, died at Kingston
upon Thames, and there buried.

25. (St. Mark's Day) Mr. Fran. Croft, in St. John Street,
my sister Edney's first husband's brother, buried y^e

27th at Clerkenwell Church.   Mr. Bell preached yᵉ funerall sermon.

27. Mr. Penning Alston, in Aldersgate Street, buried in Aldersgate Church.

26. My old Lady Hynde, mother to Sir Tho. Dayrell, died in Cambridgshire, aged 89 years.

27. My old acquaintance and once fellow clerk, and late keeper of Ludgate, Mr. John Nicols, died at his house near Welsh Poole, in Mongomeryshire.

May   5. Old Mr. Nath. Fordham died in Little Morefields.

7. Geo. Sleigh, my brother Walter's man, died in the country of a consumption.

20. Mⁱˢ Prose, the widdow and relict of Mr. Prose,ᵃ the Dutch Minister, died, and was buried May 22nd.

June.   Old Mⁱˢ Ouer, widdow of Mr. Rich. Ouer, of King's Lanley, died in London.

23. . . . . . . Dorebarre, an old carpenter in Bell Alley, in Coleman Street, died, accompted a rich man.

21. Our neighbour Sam. Chappell, in Gun Alley, who married the widdow of Mr. Wells there, died at Ely, and there buried the 23rd of June. She is since married to one . . . . . Haughton, an organist and alehouse keeper.

July.   None in July.

August.   Mr. Wm. Cham, once a sergeant in Warddow Street, died.

11. Mʳˢ Poole, wife to Mr. Matth. Poole, minister, buried at St. Andrew's, Holborn; Dr. Stillingfleet preachd.

24. (St. Bartholomew's Day) buried, my coz. Coleman's wife, comfit makers in Leadenhall St., at St. Andrew's Undershaft

24. (St. Bartholomew's Day) buried, the wife of Mr. Tho.

ᵃ He is called Proest in p. 76.—ED.

Williams, bookseller in Little Brittain, daughter to Rich. Coats, printer.

21. Dr. Waye, a physitian, died at Lambeth.

22. Geo. Hall, Bishop of Chester, once preacher at Aldersgate, died at Wiggan in Lancashire.

Septem. 29. . . . . Tibbalds, parish clerk of St. Giles's Criplegate, died; buried Friday Oct. 2 following.

Octob. 4. Mr. Geo. Townsend, confectioner wthout Aldersgate, died (whose uncle was Mr. Geo. Townsend, attorn. of Staple Inne) ; buried Octob. 8.

8. Old Mr. Smith at Islington buried.

8. Mis Atkyns, wife to Mr. Atkyn, glasier in our parish, died; buried Octob. 10.

26. *Die Lune, hora* 12 *sub nocte,* Sam. Thompson, bookseller in Duck Lane, obit. a good husband and industrious man in his profession.

Novem. 4. Mr. James Vancourt, a weaver of silke stuffs in Grub Street, died a very rich man, and of good report; buried in Criplegate church Nov. 8.

7. Mr. Looker, attorn. Comon Pleas, sometime clerk to ye Company of Bakers, died at his house at Lambeth.

16. Mis Raynes, widdow, daughter to Sir Reginald Foster, buried at Criplegate church.

26. Mr. . . . Jermin, carpenter and sawyer, buried in Criplegate church wthout a Sermon; died poore, by report.

27. Mis Sarah Peare, wife to Mr. Rich. Peare, preacher at ye Tower, died, having first buried her new born babe.

23. Mr. Norton, once a clerk for ye Commissioners of Bankrupt, died; son of Mr. Norton attorn. of the Cõmon Pleas.

Decem. 17. Mis Turlington, wife to Mr. Turlington a spectacle^a
              in Cornhill, buried.

         27. Wingfield Blackmore died at Hagerston.

Januar.   Mr. Rich. Billedg wife, uncle to Mrs Tasker, Maj^r
              Tasker's wife, buried from Lorimers' Hall in Criple-
              gate church.

Febr.   6. Tho. Dicas, bookseller, died at midnight of a consump-
              tion, much indebted. He was partner in some books
              wth Mr. Martyn and Mr. Alestry.

         10. Dr. Sam. Bolton, a prebend of Westminster, and
              preacher at St. Peter's ye Poor in Broad Street and
              at St. Martyn's L' Grand in London, died.

         11. Hen. Banister, porter of Christ's Hospital, died.

         21. On Shrove Sunday died Mr. Tho. Knowles, linnen
              draper in Holborn, near Shoe Lane.

166⅔.   1. Martyn Owen, a rich brewer w^{th}out Bishopsgate, died,
March   (his wife dying about 6 weeks before,) leaving between
              them on only son; he gave to Dr. John Owen, now
              an Independent preacher, some time Vice-Chancel-
              lor of Oxford, his kinsman, 500*li.* legacie; buried at
              St. Butolph Bishopsgate Wednesday March 10.

         17. Mis Hackett, wife to Mr. Hackett innkeeper at the
              Bell in Finsbury, died sodenly.

         20. Mr. John Crook, bookseller in Duck Lane, brother to
              Andr. Crook, died this morning; buried at Botolph's
              Aldersgate Mar. 23.

                              1669.

March   26. Cap^n Dakers, in Finsbury Lord^{sp}, the city painter, died
              this morning of a gangrene caused by cutting of a
              corne of his toe.

         26. Sir Tho. Dayrell, Kt. son to my uncle Fran. Dayrell,

              ^a *The word* maker *omitted.*—ED.

died at his house at Camps Castle in Cambridgeshire, and was buried there Apr. 5.

19. Edw. Stapleton, taylor in Covent Garden, died this night; buried Mar. 23.

April   19. Mr. Woodcock, in Grub Street, once a vintner at the Windmill in Old Jury, then in Shorditch, buried from his house in Grub Street.

21. John Borne, professor of physick at the Twyns near ye Pope's Head tavern in Great Morefields, buried.

Alice Comings, once my servant, since married to one Hodkins, at the Rose and Crown alehouse in Cursitor's Alley, died ye beginning of this month, reported to have been infected wth a foule disease by her leud husband.

May   9. Old Mis Buckley, mother to Mis Drew, wife to Mr. Drew the blacksmith in Sythes Lane, died; buried May 11.

24. Old Jones, the botcher in White's Alley in Little Morefields, an alms man of the Merchant Taylors' Company, buried.

June   4. Mr. Robt. Hurst, our brewer, at ye Hart wthout Criplegate, died this night; buried from Lorimers' Hall June 7 (*sans* Sermon).

18. Mr. Edlyn, brewer in Golding Lane, buried in Criplegate. church. Dr. Prichard preached his funerall sermon.

The same day Coll. Sheppard, a sugar baker, buried in the new church yard in Criplegate parish (as he desired).

27. Mis. Anne Ward, our neighbour Ward's wife in Little Morefields, this day died; buried in the new Church yard July 1.

July   1. Mr. Anth. Sambrook, in Bell Alley in Coleman Street, of the East India Company, hanged himself.

July   3. Mⁱˢ Gunthorp, in Morefields, the widdow of Mr. Gun-
thorpe, sword-bearer to yᵉ Lord Mayor, died in
Morefields.

20. Mⁱˢ Wharton, wife to Dr. Wharton in Morefields, died
hor. 10 *ante merid.* buried in a vault in St. Michael
Basheshaw July 23.

24. My cosen Rebecca Owen, widdow, buried from her
house in New King Street in High Holborn at St.
Giles in the Fields.

23. Majʳ Fran. Nicolls, Surveyor of yᵉ Ordinance in the
Tower, died this night *hora xi. sub nocte* at the
Tower; buried at St. Clement's wᵗʰout Temple
Barr (Mr. Gifford preached) July 26.

27. Mⁱˢ Anne Noblet, widdow, some time the mother of
John Tredway of Hagerston, dying at Shorditch,
was buried from Lorimers' Hall in Criplegate church;
her daughter Robinson was her executrix.

29. William Cade, alderman's deputy, wᵗʰout Bishopsgate,
died; a wise, pious, and charitable citizen.

Old John Clark, bookseller under Creechurch (once in
Cornhill), my old acquaintance, died this day, *plenus
dierum et senij infirmitatum.*

24. *Hora* 1ᵐᵃ *sub nocte* Mr. John Turlington, spectacle
maker in Cornhill, my old acquaintance, died.

August   3. Mr. Charles Helmes, Preacher in White's Alley in
Little Morefields, some time preacher at Winchcomb
in Gloucestershire, died; buried at Bedlam yᵉ 6.

4. Mr. Heddy, poulterer in Forestreet, buried at Criplegate; Mr. Welbanck preacher.

5. Mⁱˢ Pickering, wife to Mr. Pickering mercer in Paternoster Row, buried at St. Butolph's Aldersgate.

6. Dr. Worth, Bp. of Killeloo in Ireland, buried in Bread
Street. Dr. Hackett, an Irish dean, preached at his
funerall.

August 6. Mis Sarah Chiswell, wife of Mr. Rich. Chiswell bookseller
in Little Brittain, buried at St. Butolph's Aldersgate;
Mr. Stoning preached.

13. Mrs Waller, wife to Captn Waller in White Cross
Street, once Mrs Work, a widdow of the lame Hospitall by Smithfield, died *hora* 1ma *sub nocte.*

14. Mr. Tho. Gunrey, secondary of ye Treasurer Remembrancer's office in the Exchequer, buried at Great
St. Bartholomew's; his only daughter, a virgin, sole
executrix.

Sept. 6. Mis Cauthorn, wife to Capt. Cauthorn stationer in New
Cheapside, buried from Lorimers' Hall.

7. Mr. Tho. Pierson, son to Mr. Pierson in Little Morefields, buried from Lorimers' Hall.

11. Old Mr. Sankey (sometime belonging to the Exchequer), dwelling against ye Charter House, died.

20. Richard Smith, once a Sergeant at the Compter in
Wood Street, now ye husband to Mrs Lincoln some
time the wife of William Lincoln, once my clerk in
the Poultry Counter, died *hora* 12 *in medio nocte*:
buried from St. Bartholomew's Hospitall Sept. 23:
myselfe, my daughter Hacker, daug. Smith, and
daugh. Edney invited to her funerall.

22. Mis Hutchins, wife to Mr. Hutchins, once of Criplegate parish, now dwelling at Hallywell, once widdow
of Mr. Pepper, a mealeman, and before of Mr.
Nightingall; buried from Lorimers' Hall in St. Giles
Church; Dr. Slater preached.

24. Sir Richard Browne, late alderman and Lord Mayor of
London, died at his house in Essex, near Saffron
Walden.

30. Mrs Elizabeth Pyers, wife to Mr. Pyers, apothecary
in Grub Street, and daughter to Mr. Wm. Newbold,

buried at St. Olave's in ye Old Jury from Lorimers' Hall.

Octob.   1. Mr. Lockyer's child, a boy, buried this day, my daug. and my daught^r^ Smith invited to ye buriall.

       1. Dr. Hen. King, Bp. of Chichester, died in Sussex.

       8. Deputy Arnold (late of Ludgate Hill), buried this day from Cookes Hall in Aldersgate Street.

    21. Mr. John Sanders (free of ye Grocers' Company), once a silkeman at the Hare in Cheapside, since an alderman (fined), one of ye Masters of Christ's Hospitall, buried from Ironmongers' Hall in Fanchurch Street to St. Peter's Church in Cheapside, died rich.

    23. Mr. Wm. Prynn, barrester of Lincoln's Inne, died.

Novem.   Sir Geo. Benyon, Kt. died ye begining of this month.

    17. Old Mr. Carter, warder at ye Tower, died.

    18. Tim. Garthwait, bookseller in Bartholomew's lame Hospitall, died; buried ye 20 w^th^out any sermon.

    20. Dr. Porey, a prebend of Paul's, reported a rich prelate &c. died this day.

    17. Mr. Rich. Procter, master in Chancery, once a pleader in the Excheq^r^ and a competitor wth Mr. Bradshaw for the Judge's place in Guildhall, died.

       About this time Mrs Elizabeth Atkinson, widdow to Atkinson ye carpenter in Grub Street, died in ye country; a good churchwoman.

       Saterday 4, *hora* 12, *merid.* John Howe, clerk of ye Exigents to Mr. Leigh, secondary of Wood Street Compter, died at his house in Aldersgate Street.

Decem.   24. Mrs Kingston, widdow, the relict of Fœlix Kingston, an antient printer in London, buried this day in Shoreditch Church, in wch parish she died Decem. 22.

    23. Widdow May, in Goswell Street, once nurse to my

cousen Hazelwood, there buried this day at St. Butolph's Aldersgate.

23. Mr. Staveley, son in law to Justice Smith of Criplegate parish, buried in St. Giles Criplegate.

17. Old Mr. Tho. Latham, once attor. in ye Ld Mayor's Court, buried in Essex; 90 years.

25. Hen. Wollaston, once keeper of Newgate, died this night in ye Charterhouse, where he was an alderman, and ther buried.

Januar.   3. Geo. Monke, Duke of Albermarle, died this morning at his house against White Hall, much lamented; his funeral from Somerset House to Westminster, Saturday Apr. 20th following.

6. Old Sir Gilbert Gerrard died at Harrow on ye Hill.

23. Sunday the Dutchess of Albemarle died, about *hora* 9 *ante merid.*

21. At or neare this day died Mr. Fletcher of Jamaica House, behinde Shoreditch, once a comfit maker in Wood Street; the best chiscake-maker.

1669-70.

Mar.   4. The Lady Brackley, wife to the Lord Brackley, son to the Earl of Bridgwater, died after she was delivered of a dead female child.

Febr.   Mr. French, our baker in More Lane, died about midnight, being well the day before.

March   22. Old goodwife Jones, in White's Alley, aged 85 years, died.

22. Daniel Fordham's wife, our trayned soldier, hempbeater in More Fields, died.

1670.

March   28. Matth. Beadle, Mr. Beadle's only son, the chandler in

Little Morefields, *hora* 4 *po. merid.* died; buried y^e
31. in New Church yard.

April   27. Mr. Tho. Juice, vicar of King's Langley in Hartford-
shire, died.

May   2. Mr. Finch, in Petty France by Bedlam, died; buried
May 6.

      5. Sir Geffry Palmer, the King's attorn. died.

      5. Edwd Earl of Manchester, Lord Chamberlain of y^e
King's household, died, aged 69 years.

May   11. Mis Heath, a tripe-wife, this Wednesday last, in her
markett by Honey Lane, at the soddain fall of a new
house ther, whereby 3 men were killed outright;
she was thereupon struck to the heart wth a trem-
bling fear, as she dyed thereof on Sunday last, and
buried this day in Criplegate church.

   11. Moses Pitt, the only child of Moses Pitt bookseller in
Little Brittain, was this day buried.

   30. Dr. Edw. Wattehouse, our familiar old acquaintance,
died this Munday morning at his house on Mile End
Green, having preached the Sunday seavenight before in London, leaving 2 little daughters behind
him: he was buried on Thursday June 2nd, at
Greenford in Middx. where he had some estate in
land; he came from thence sick on Monday May 23,
in Whitson week, after he had preached at Finchley
on Whitsonday, unto Mile End, where he died, as
above.

   31. Mr. Blofeild, a Norfolk minister, died at his house in
Norfolk.

June   2. Dr. Nathan. Hardy, Dean of Rochester, reported to
have died at his house at Croydon.

    7. Mr. John Robinson, cordwayner (who married Mr.
Tredway's daughter), buried from Armourers' Hall
in Criplegate church; wth ticketts.

4. Mr. Drew, blacksmith in St. Sythes Lane, died;
buried ye 7th; w^thout ticketts.

11. Old Mrs Shute, the widdow of Mr. Jos. Shute preacher,
died, aged above 100 years.

16. My coz. Mary Dayrell, the elder of ye 2 daught^rs of
Sir Tho. Dayrell, died in Holborn at 2 of ye clock
in the morning, of ye small pox.

19. Henrietta Maria, sister to our Soveraign K. Charles y^e
2nd, and wife to the D. of Orleance, brother to y^e
King of France, died at Clou near Paris; she was
struck sick sodenly on Sunday, and died on Monday
morn.

22. Old Mr. Lawrence, an apothecary in Cheapside, near
the great condict, buried.

July   15. Philemon Stephens, bookseller in Chancery Lane, died
at Chelsey; buried at St. Dunstan's in ye West.

15. Sir John Wolstenhalm, son of Sir Jo. Wolstenhalm,
Kt., of the Custom House, buried at Stanmore in
Middx. The Lady Corbett coming to visit him,
being her uncle, fell sick and died, and buried w^th
him.

21. Meacham, sexton of St. Giles' Criplegate, died this
morning by a fall (on Thursday July 14th) from a
wall by the Windmills in Moorefields into a ditch
beneath, from whence he, lying a sleep, fell down,
and was deadly bruised; buried Friday 22nd; M^r
Welbanck the lecturer preached at his burial.

24. Cozen Peak, widdow, allyed to Sir Tho. Dayrell, died
at my cozen Mary Dayrell's in St. Giles' parish in y^e
Fields.

29. Mr. Edward Fleetwood's wife, a belt maker in King
Street, Westminster, died, being brought to bed on
Munday before.

August   5. This night Dr. Richard Pierson, a civilian, brother to John Pierson Dr. D. died at Mr. Smith's house, an apothecary in Little Britain (of a surfeit, as is conjectured), having lyen sick not above four or five dayes.

11. Mⁱˢ Fleetwood, mother to Mr. Fleetwood yᵉ belt maker in King Street at Westminster, buried this day at Westminster, where she died.

23. Richard Banks, attorn. of the King's Bench, once an attorn. at Guildhall, London, died at his house in Bishopsgate Street.

25. Old Mr. Mills, the city bricklayer, buried from Grocers' Hall.

29. Mr. Edw. Trotman, secondary of yᵉ Poultry Compter, died at Hackney; buried Sept. 7, in St. Margarett's Loathbury, in the ruines of yᵉ chancell, in a vault; his corps brought from Grocers' Hall. His eldest son, Edw. Trotman, was sworn secondary in his father's roome, Septʳ 6, at Guildhall.

Sept.   14. Mⁱˢ Mary Mynn, wife to Mr. John Myn, grocer wᵗʰout Aldersgate, died at 2 o'clock in the morning; buried Septʳ 17.

13. Mr. Rich. Hurleston, of Redrith, merchᵗ, (my brother Walter's acquaintance, and debtor to me in 300*li.*) buried there; he died Sept. 4.

28. Mr. Austin, deputy of Aldersgate Street Ward wᵗʰin, near Goldsmith Hall, buried.

28. Mr. Birkhead, brasier in Cornhill, buried.

Octobʳ   4. Alderman Ridges, sometime a salesman at the end of Long lane in Smithfield; buried wᵗʰ a pompous funerall at St. Pulchers church, a very rich man.

25. Mr. Covill, a goldsmith, his corps carried from Cloathworkers' Hall to Chealsey, there to be interred; it is reported that he died indebted above four hundred thousand pound, and had an estate to satisfie his

creditors to a penny, and a very great estate overplus.

Novem. 3. *Die Jovis hora* 8ª *ante merid. obijt Jacob. Allestry, Bibliopola in Cœmiter. D. Pauli Lond. sepult. Lunœ* 7 *Nov. Fitz-Williams capellan. Episcop. Winton. concionem facit funeb.*

13. *Die Dominica, circa hora* 6. *post merid. obijt Hum. Robinson, Bibliopola Trium Columb. in Cœmiter. D. Pauli, reliquens unum fil. et unam filiam. Sepult. in ruinis Eccles. S. Fidei sub. ecclesiam Cathedr. D. Pauli die Lunœ* 21 *Nov.* 1670.

12. Died Jane Harris in child bed at her house in the Strand, who (being sister to Anne Vize) was once my servant.

25. The wife of Mr. Broome, once my wives taylor, died; buried 26 Novr 1670.

Decem. 1. Peter Dayrell, an infant of 6 or seven weeks old, y^e
Thursday. first begotten child of my cozen Paul Dayrell, sonn of my cozen Peter Dayrell, late of Lillingston Dayrell, died in Little Brittaine this day; Decem. 3 buried in St. Butolph w^thout Aldersgate.

Decem. 7. William Barrett, a baker in Criplegate parish, died;
Wednesday. buried ye Friday following.

29. Tho. Tunman, deputy of ye Ward of Farringdon w^thout,
Thursday. father in law to Theophil. Smith, woollen draper, was this day buried.

30. James Flesher, printer, son in law to Cornelius Bee,
Friday. bookseller, died at Clarkenwell.

January.

Februa. 1. Old Meg Large, some time my servant, the wife of
Wednesday. old Large, a very poor man at the Spittle near Shoreditch, died this day.

7. Sir John Ray, Kt. late of Richmond, once a scrivener
Tuesday in Fleet Street, buried this day.

Mond.

20. My cozen Peter Dayrell, son and heire of his father Peter Dayrell, late of Lillingstone Dayrell in Bucks, died there w^{th}out issue; buried there Friday Feb. 4. The mannor of Lillingston was left to . . . . (the son of Ant. Dayrell, minister of Lillingston) upon under age, to enter into possession when he shall be of full age. Paul and Richard Dayrell, bretheren to Peter Dayrell, his executors, in the mean time to hold possession of ye lordship, and to receive ye proffits thereof, deducting out of the same debts, legacies, costs, &c. as the land was lyable to.

March

21. Tuesday, Mary Walter, widdow, mother to John Walter, baker at Layton Buzzard, son in law to my sister Edney, died at her son Beadle's, mealeman, in Shorditch.

30. Lambert Godfrey, once recorder of Maidston, eldest son of Mr. Tho. Godfrey of Kent, by his first wife, died this day; buried at Westminster April 1 following.

31. Anne Dutchess of York, daughter to ye Earl of Clarendon, sometime Lord Chancellor of England, wife to James Duke of York, brother to K. Charles ye 2nd, died this day.

31. Friday, Sir John Dethick, late alderman, who was Sheriff 1649 and Mayor of London 1655, died this day.

1671.

April

4. Robert Lant, in Finsbury, merch^t (whose wife and relict was sister to Sir Tho. Dayrell by the mother, but daur. of Eusebius Andrews, Esqr, dying in childbed). Y^e said Robt. Lant died Mar. 23, and was this day buried from Drapers' Hall at St. Peter's ye Poore in Broadstreet, where Dr. Orton preached his funerall sermon. I had a ring at ye buriall.

7. Penyell Bowen, stationer, once apprentice to Octavian Pulleyn, sen[r], bookseller in St. Paul's Church Yard, dying of a veyne broken, was buried at St. Butolph's w[th]out Aldersgate.

17. Monday. Thom. Williams, eldest son of Thomas Williams, bookseller in Little Brittain, this day dyed at his Lodgings at Tottenham of a consumption.

24. Dr. Chr. Shute, D.D. son of N. Shute once minister at St. Mildred Poultry, died this day, and was buried in y[e] parish of St. Foster, in Foster Lane, where he was preacher.

May. Mr. John Agar, attorn. Comon Pleas, died about this time, and was buried at Barnes in Surrey; he married the daughter of Mr. Thom. Squire, preacher at Shoreditch.

5. Edw. Montague, Earl of Manchester, Lord Chamberlain of the King's Houshold, died about midnight of y[e] collick, being pretty well and abroad y[e] day before.

10. Sir John Kelling, Kt. Lord Chief Justice of the King's Bench, died this day, being y[e] first day of Easter Term, about 2 o'clock in y[e] morning.

11. John Payne, attorn. in y[e] Excheq[r] in y[e] King's Remembrancer's Office, died; buried May 16.

13. Sir John Langham, sometime alderman and sheriff of London 1642, died, aged 88 years.

June 4. Rich. Fleetwood, eldest son of his father Jeffry Fleetwood, and of his mother Anne Fleetwood, my daughter, died, and buried at the Tower on Tuesday next following.

19. Tho. Bourne, bookseller at Bedlam (my old acquaintance), died *hora* 8 *p[t]. merid.*; his corps carried from Lorimers' Hall to Bottol. Bishopsgate, Thurs. June 22, and there buried, with the service of the Common Prayer, though he died a Recusant.

21. Woodward, keeper of Newgate, buried from Lorimer Hall.

22. Anne Giffard, wife of Mr. . . . . . Giffard, keeper of ye Poultry Compter (after a long and tedious sickness), died this day, buried Saterday June 24.

28. Elizabeth Calcott, a young child, ye younger daughter of my cozen Dorothy Calcott, daughter to my brother Walter Smith, died at Richmond.

July

4. Mr. Cole, haberdasher, once my cosen John Houlker's master, buried.

24. Fr. Mitchell, clerk-sitter of ye Poultry Comptor, died July 19 at his lodging in Jewen Street, and his corps was this day carried from London to Reading, and was there buried; a good clerk and an honest man; Mr. Lloyd of Reading preached at his buriall, ye sermon is printed.

17. Maj^r Cox, muster-master-generall for ye city of London, died this day.

August

7. Daniell Trotman, younger brother of Edw. Trotman, secondary of ye Poultry Compter, coming wth some company from Hackney, calling in by ye way at ye Verginia Alehouse to play a little at ye board's end, was sodenly taken wth a vomiting of blood, and again p^esently vomiting againe, at least a quart more of blood, therewithall fell downe speechless, and some imposture or vein (as is conjectured) breaking in him and choaking him; buried August 10th at Lothbury Church.

8. Mr. Webb, once a Reader at St. Giles Criplegate, this day died (with report of no good husband).

23. Mr. Selfe, carpenter in Butler's Alley, tenant to Mr. Trotman, was this day buried in the New Church Yard beyond the Wind mills.

22. Sir Rich. Riues, alderman in election (by course) to have beene Lord Mayor this next year, died this day.

12. Mr. Rich. Tisdale died in Clerkenwell, and was there this day buried; he was son of Mr. Rich. Tisdale, once clerk of yᵉ papers in Wood Street Compter.

Septem. 10. Francis Webb, once a scrivener in Cornhill, died at his house in Oxford Street.

17. Susana Fleetwood, widdow, late wife of Tho. Fleetwood, gentl. buried this night in Bermondsey Church.

Octob. 4. The wife of John Spencer, keeper of yᵉ library at Sion Colledge, buried at St. Alphage.

5. Goodwife King, wife of John King of yᵉ ffarme at King's Langley in Hertfordshire, buried.

10. Mr. Goad, a fellow of Eaton Colledge, buried.

Novem. 23. Wm. Lincoln, younger son of Wm. Lincoln once my clerk in the Poultry Compter, buried at Little St. Bartholomew's by Smithfield, where his mother, Mⁱˢ Smith, a widdow, dwelt.

23. Mr. Herbert, apothecary in yᵉ Minories, died; buried Nov. 26.

Decem. 1. Mr. Clinton's 2nd wife, a silk dyer in Coleman Street, died; buried Munday 4th following in the burial place beyond the Artillery Garden.

19. Mr. Clinton's daughter Anne, by a former wife, aged about 4 yeares, buried in yᵉ same place.

January 2. Mr. Cornelius Bee, bookseller in Little Brittain, died *hora* xiˢ. *ante merid.* his 2 eldest daughters, Mⁱˢ Norwood and Mⁱˢ Fletcher, widdows, executrixes; buried Jan. 4 at Great St. Bartholomew's, wᵗʰout a sermon, wᵗʰout wine or waffers, only gloves and rosmary; Dr. Wells of Aldersgate read yᵉ service. His younger daughter married to Nath. Hook, his servant.

15. Dr. John Cosin, Bp. of Durham, died near Charing Cross, *circa hora* 4 *pⁱ. merid.*

24. Magdalen Price, *alias* Rogers, burnt in Smithfield for cliping money, in Tenter Alley in Little More fields.

Februa.   3. Mr. Bromfield, merchant in Coleman Street, died very wealthy, having fined for alderman; buried in St. Antholin's Church Feb. 15.

9. Mr. Avery, town clerk, died; buried privatly.

9. Mr. Fox in Smithfield, buried, a rich man, having fined for alderman.

17. Sir Geo. Tash died at his house near Uxbridge, in whose house my coz. Kath. Houlker once was servant.

20. Mr. Clarke of Finsbury, a rich batchellor of the Drapers' Company, buried at St. Andrew's Undershaft; Dr. Prichard made his fune^ll sermon.

21. Old Dr. Tho. Reeve, my old acquaintance, who preached at my son John's buriall, died this day at Waltham Abbey.

16. Dr. Robt. Britten, minister of Ludgate and Deptford, a good schollar and preacher, died this night at Deptford w^thin 2 hours after he fell ill.

15. Deputy Garford, in Hounsditch in Aldgate Ward, father in law to alderman Starling, whose wife was the Deputies only child, died.

167½.

March   8. Richard Peare, preacher at ye Tower, died about midnight, buried the 9 Mar.

11. Mr. Bushrope a Frenchman, apothecary, died this day in Redcross Street.

6. Tho. Lucas, the oldest Sergeant of ye Poultry Compter, died; buried Mar. 9.

11. Dr. Henchman, vicar of Christ Church in London, kinsman to Dr. Henchman, Bp. of London, died at Chigwell in Essex; buried at Christ Church Munday 18.

18. Old Mr. Marsh, store keeper of ye Tower, died aged 83 years; buried ye 22.

21. Mis Luckyn, wife to Mr. Luckyn, once parish clerk of Criplegate; buried in Criplegate Church.

1672.

April   5. (Good Friday). Mr. Farley, once a grocer in St. Peter's Wood Street, died at Islington; there buried.

4. Dr. Bolles, a learned physician, buried from his house in ye Strand in a court on this side of the May Pole, on the left side of the Strand.

8. Mr. Anthony Dowse, stationer in Little Brittain, died this day before noone; buried at St. Butolph's Aldersgate ye 13th. Dr. Meriton preached at his funerall.

11. This night Mr. Brand died, an old stocking seller in Barbican, of a blow given him on his head (the day before) at a coffee house in Barbican by one Kitchen wth an earthen drinking pott or jugg, as is commonly reported.

18. This morning died Sir Johnathan Dawes, one of the Sheriffs of London; and one Friday, ye next day, chosen in his place for ye residue of ye year Alderman . . . . Moore, grocer.

May   8. Moses Pitt buried his young and only daughter and child at St. Butolph's Aldersgate.

16. (Ascention Day). The funerall of Sir Johnathan Dawes, late Sheriff of London, from Fishmongers' Hall to Cree Church, and there interred.

June   12. Ellen Smith, the first and only child and daught^r of my cozen Walter Smith (son of my brother Walter Smith), died at Richmond.

30. This Sunday in the afternoone died John Smith, alderman of London and justice of peace in Middlesex, at his house in Finsbury; his funerall the 16th July from Goldsmiths' Hall to Criplegate Church, where he was interred, with a sermon by Dr. Prichard our vicar. The posie of his rings, "Ever Last." He made a great gaine by musk catts which he kept.

July 10. Robt. Prichard, our sexton, died about 7 of ye clock in ye afternoone; buried ye 12.

13. Herbert Thorndike, prebend of Westminster, buried at Westminster.

21. Samuel Crumbleholme, schoolmaster of Paul's School, died; buried ye 26. Dr. Wells of Aldersgate preached his funerall sermon at my Lord Mayor's Chapell by Guildhall. Rings were given, whose posie was, *Redime Tempus.*

Mr. . . . . Nedham, bookseller in Little Brittain, died.

August 2. Matthew Barker, once an attorn. of the Guildhall, died at the house of Mr. Finch, a mercer in the Minories, whose wife was Mr. Barker's daughter, having a long time lyen distempered wth a dead palsie, which befell him in August 1668; the funerall was the 15th, from Turners' Hall in Philpot Lane to St. Butolph's Aldersgate, where he was interred. Mr. Chr. Flower preached.

23. Mr. . . . . Wall, who had fined for Alderman, buried, who was a wollen draper at ye west end of Paul's.

Septem. 5. Sir Andrew Riccard, once alderman and sheriff of London, died very wealthy, leaving one only daughter behind him, who was married to my Lord Berkley; his funerall to St. Olave's Crutched Friars Septr 17.

Dr. Francklyn, phisitian of ye Tower, buried.

11. Mr. Wm. Over, of Chipperfield, in King's Langley, Hertfordshire, buried.

25. Mr. . . . . Leak, fishmonger w^thin Criplegate, died; buried Octob. 2d.

Octob^r. 11. Leticia Calcott, daughter of my cosen Dorothy Calcott (my brother Walter's daughter), died at Richmond, to ye great grief of her grandfather, as well of her parents and other allies, haven lyen sick about 3 weeks.

27. John Bulkley, a wholesale grocer, allied to Betty and Nan. Hacker, buried this day, who fell sick of a violent, burning feavor but 2 or 3 dayes before.

Novem. 12. Old Dr. John Frier, (phisitian) in Little Britain, died, aged 96 years; buried Novem. 19th.

9. Old Sir Tho. Player, Chamberlain of London, died.

7. Old Mr. Roger Reves, oyleman on Snow Hill, his funerall to St. Pulcher's Church from Sadlers' Hall in Cheapside; his wife died Decemb. 5th following; buried Decem. 9 at St. Pulcher's. They had 5 sons and 6 daughters living, and 60 mourners.

11. John Reynolds, seedsman Old Jury, Colechurch parish, died.

17. Old John Padwick, packthred maker in Little More Fields, died this morning.

Decem. 26. Mr. Crofton, a preacher, buried at St. Buttolp Aldersgate. Dr. Arden, rector there, preached at his funerall.

January. Mr. Wells, bookseller in Little Brittain, (my old acquaintance,) died this Satterday morning; buried at St. Butolph's ext. Aldersgate Jan. No sermon.

The famous cheat (commonly called ye German Princess) hanged at Tyborn (wth others) at a generall execution.

Mis Williams, wife to Mr. Williams wollen draper in Fleet Street, and daughter to Mr. Jones comon councell man, buried.

20. Robert Leigh, Esqr. of Gray's Inne, father to Mis Hacker, wife to Mr. John Hacker, eldest brother to my son Hacker, buried this day.

Feb. 8. Old Mis Katherine Johnson, mother to Mrs Winch in

Grub Street, died this day; buried 14th at St.
James' Garlick Hith, wth a sermon by Dr. Buck.

Feb^r.   12. Old Wm. Leake, stationer wthin Temple Barr in Fleet
Street, buried.

25. Old Mis Bowyer, widdow, aged 86 years Nov. 6 last,
buried in St. Mildred's Church in ye Poultry, where
her husband Mr. Wm. Bowyer *alias* Gamble, vintner at ye Rose, sometime lived. She died in Covent
Garden.

March 16th. Mis Rothwell, mother to Mr. James Rothwell of y^e
Tower of London, died this day in Lancashire, where
she dwelt.

23. Old John Nicolson, a poore man, once a station^r, well
acquainted wth all the booksellers, died this night,
having been abroad ye afternoone before. Some report he starved himselfe through miserableness, tho'
since his death there was money sufficiently found, by
him, to have satisfied his wants.

1673.

March   25. James Ince, parish clerk of St. Butol. Aldergate, died.

April   2nd. Mr. John Looker, clerk of ye Company of Coopers,
buried at St. Martyn's wthin Ludgate, from Coopers'
Hall in Basinghall Street: his wife was daughter to
Mr. John Nicolls keeper of Ludgate: he died Mar. 28.
.   No sermon, but rings, engraven, I. L. obit Mar. 28.

29. Dr. Horton, preacher at St. Ellen's within Bishopsgate,
buried.

April   2. This day died Old Mr. Tho. Browne, grocer, (comonly
called Ruff Browne,) who had fined for Alderman,
at his new house in Watling Street, whither he
lately went out of Old Street wthout Criplegate, 3
dayes after he went thither; buried ye 7. Mr.

Durham, minister of St. Mildred's Bread Street,
preached.

10. Mis Siday, a midwife at London Wall (well known),
whose aunt and mother's sister was old Mis Hutchinson in the Poultry, our old acquaintance, died.

10. Mr. Edmond Arnold the younger, only son of Mr. Edmond Arnold of Drs Comons, buried this day at All-
hallowes Lombard Street.

19. Old Mr. Bilbon, bricklayer of St. Giles' Criplegate,
bountifull to the poor in his life time, buried.

25. John Bolton, once Mr. Pet. Ladore's man, now a chandler in Grub Street, buried.

22. Nathaniel Hooke, bookseller in Little Brittain, who
married ye youngest daught^r of Corn. Bee, died this
day about one a clock at noone at Stanmore, and
was buried on Thursday April 24 following.

Old Hyde, bookseller in Jewen Street, buried.

June 18. Alderman John Smith, salter in Bread Street, died,
dives opum ; he was sheriff wth Jam. Edwards, grocer,
Mich'as 1669; his funerall from Drapers' Hall to
St. Mary Aldermanbury Church July 17.

July 15. The wife of Pelham Moore, vintner within More gate,
died; an old, infirm woman.

27. Mr. Tho. Broome, an old Sergeant at law, died.

August. Potter, of Criplegate parish, buried Aug. 4.

7. John Smith, son of Ant. Maria Smith, herald painter,
died at Chelsey, and buried ye 20th at St. Dunstan's
in the West, *cœlebs.* Mr. Fra. Smith of Hurst in
Berkshire was his unckle.

18. Sir Geo. Viner, Kt. and his lady, their funer^ll from
Hackney to St. Mary Wolneth in Lombard Street,
wth great pomp.

Septem. 2. Dr. Perencheif, minister of St. Mildred's Poultry and a
Prebend of Westminster, buried at Westminster
this night.

Septem. 12. *Hora* 8ª *ante merid. Domina Anna Forster, uxor Reginaldi Forster milit. p'och. St. Egid' extra Criplegate (guttarÿ ip'ius secundæ) interfecit; sepulta die Jovis* 18 *die Septemb. in p'och. St. Helenæ intra Bishopsgate.*

17. Old Mⁱˢ Wheller (who once dwelt at the Hercules near Bone Hill) died in yᵉ parish of St. Giles Criplegate.

19. Mr. Dell, of Criplegate parish, gingerbread seller, died; was buried yᵉ 24th, wᵗʰ no good fame.

     Mr. Lane, on of yᵉ comon councell of yᵉ city of London, died.

18. Jane, the wife of John Scott, our chymney sweeper, buried.

Octobʳ. This month died Mⁱˢ Underhill, wife to Cave Underhill, a stage player in Salisbury Court, once wife to Thomas Robinson, vintner in Cheapside.

12. Mr. Lawrence, brewer in Red Cross Street, died; buried Octʳ 14.

14. Mr. Archer, merchᵗ in Morefields, by Rope Makers' Alley, died.

Novem. 10. John Walters, baker in Black Fryers, my sister Edney's son in law, died, and buried yᵉ 11; he sickned yᵉ day before.

14. *Circa meridiem noctis obijt Tho. Wharton, Med. Doct.* [*apud*] *ædes suas in Aldersgate Street, fama optima; sepult. in ruinis Ecclesiæ S. Mich. Bassishaw, ubi quondam inhabitavit, die Jovis, Nov.* 20. *De Religione hujus Medici fama diversa.*

20. Sarah Ward, the only daughter of Mr. Ward, butcher in Criplegate parish, buried, who died Nov. 17.

23. Died the wife of my cozen Richard Dayrell, stockinseller in the Strand; buried in St. Mary Savoy Church Nov. 27.

24. Rich. Minors, head beadle of Drapers' Hall, died this day, and was buried at St. Peter's yᵉ Poore Nov. 27.

29. Mr. Wm. Sanchey, goldsmith in Rope Makers' Alley,

in Little Morefields, died; buried at St. Giles' Criplegate Decem. 2nd.

Decemb. 1. Mr. . . . . . Stanneir, of Bednall Green, florist, buried at Great St. Ellen's, London.

31. Dr. Ch^r Fearn, Med. D. died at his house in Lime Street.

This month old Nicolls, ye cobler in Coleman Street, died.

January 6. Emanuel Davis died, hattband maker in White's Alley in Little Morefields; buried in ye New Church Yard beyond the New Artillery Ground Jan. 8.

23. Edw. Sparkes, a clerk in an office in the Tower, died this day; buried in the Minories ye 25th.

18. Old Tho. Large, late husband to Margarett, once my maid servant, buried at St. Buttol. Bishopsgate; died in Half Moone Alley in Bishopsgate Street, a very poore alms man.

Febru. 12. James Mayo, attorn. Comon Pleas, and Clerk of the Warrants, died at his house in Chancery Lane, aged about 84 years; buried Feb. 17.

14. Elizabeth, ye elder of the 2 twynnes of my coz. Dor. Calcott, died this day at her nurse's at Richmond; born at my brother house on Ludgate Hill Jany 20th.

25. Samuel Simons, in Shorditch, a bayliff of Midd. and vitler, buried. He was robbed by those theeves who robbed me about ye same time.

167¾.

March 1. Samuell Man, bookseller, aged about 87, died this morning in Ive Lane. He was formerly apprentice to Mr. Welby, bookseller in St. Paul's Church Yard.

March 5. Mis Jane Whittle, wife to Mr. Tho. Whittle, of Red Cross Street, strongwater man, this day died (a good friend of mine), of good report; buried Mar. 10th in St. Giles' parish, wth a sermon, made by Mr. Smithies o^r lecturer.

1674.

April   4. At 10 in the forenoon died old Mr. Church, once a scrivener, at his house in Tenter Alley in Little Morefields.

18. Major John Grant of Birching Lane, died of yᵉ jaunios; buried April 22 in St. Dunstan's in yᵉ West (as is reported) a Roman Catholick ; an understanding man, of a quick witt and a pretty schollar, my old acquaintance.

18. Mr. Rich. Meridale, once a scrivener, and an attorn. of yᵉ Comon Pleas (near yᵉ Charterhouse), died this night in Barbican, Criplegate parish (noe friend of my sister Edney's).

11. Mˡˢ Jacomb, wife to Dr. Jacomb (once minister of St. Martyn's Ludgate,) who died April 8th at the Countess of Exeter's house in Little Brittain, and was buried from thence Apr. 11.

28. Mr. Joseph Clarke, once Mr. Tim. Garthwait's apprentice, bookseller in Little Brittain, buried.

May   8. Auditor Beale, in Hatton Garden, cast himselfe out of his upper window (as is by most believed) into his yard, of which fall he died imediately, the moving cause unknown. He had a wife and 2 children living. He died worth a great estate in lands and monies. Some pretend that it was by accident, others through frenzie, wherewith otherwiles he was possessed, whereof the coroner's enquest found that he perished by throwing himselfe downe in his frantick fitt.

Dr. Sabastian Smith, a prebend of Christ Church in Oxford, eldest son to my unckle Edw. Smith, died this month.

June   11. Mary Winston, wife to Edw. Winston, carpenter in Beech Lane in Criplegate parish, died about midnight (St. Barnabas' Day); buried in Criplegate parish June 14. Mr. Smithers preached; my sister Edney, Betty and Nan. Hacker only of our family invited to ye buriall, my daugh^t Hacker being at Eaton.

July 23. Hen. Neason, son of . . . . Neason (a porter), brother in law to my sister Edney, who died at St. Bartholomew's Hospitall; buried from thence this day.

August 7. Died, Mis Anne Badger, wife of Mr. Allen Badger of Hagerston, near Hoggesdon, in the parish of St. Leonard Shorditch; buried Aug. 11th. Dr. Hatfield preached on Psalm 144, 4 ver. my daughter Hacker (only of our family invited) had a ring at her buriall.

August. About this time died Serenus Cressey in Sussex; he wrote and published ye Church History of Brittaine in folio, 1668.

22. Mis Mary Leigh, wife to Mr. Edw. Leigh, secondary of Wood Street Compter, died in childbed of a male child, the 7th child of 4 males and 3 females; her funerall was carried from her house in Great St. Bartholomew's where she died, to Ivor near Uxbridg to be buried.

Septem. 11. Bridget Underwood, a young maid who came out of Gloucestershire to London wth our maid Kate Butter to gett her a service, dying of the small pox at her unckle's in the Strand, this day buried.

20. Andrew Crooke, bookseller, this evening died, being well the day before among his acquaintance in Little Brittain; my old acquaintance.

23. My cosen Windham Dayrell, 3rd son of my cosen Sir Thom. Dayrell, died this night.

30. About 7 or 8 in the morning died at the Tower, old Mr. Talbot Edwards, keeper of ye Crowne and other of his Maj^{ties} Jewells under Sir Gilbert Talbot, Master of

the King's Jewell house, aged about 78 years, some say 80; buried in St. Peter's Church in the Tower, Oct. 1. Mr. Giffard of St. Dunstan's in ye East made his funerall sermon.

Octob^r. 4. Mr. Wm. Lorrindg, confectioner, died at his house in the country.

Novem. 15. John Milton died at Bunhill near Morefields in Criplegate parish, blind some time before he died.

9. Died at Rouen in France Sir Edward Hide, Earl of Clarendon, once Lord Chancellor of England, in place succeeded Sir Orlando Bridgman, Lord Keeper; buried at Westminster, Munday Jan. 4, 1674.

4. Buried in Criplegate Church old Thomas Came, a taylor, from his house in Jewen Street, formerly dwelling in Wood Street, where I long since knew him to be a journyman of Criplegate Ward.

18. Mis Dionysia Jones, wife of deputy Jones, buried this day from Lorimers' Hall at St. Giles w^{th}out Criplegate; my daughter Hacker and sister Edney had tickets and gold rings.

21. Died Thomas Quarterman, parish clerk of St. Giles Criplegate; buried the 23rd, to whose buriall I was invited.

Decem. 15. Died my cosen Wicks, sister to my cosen Paul Dayrell, at her house at Lillingston Dayrell, Bucks.

Januar. 1. My Lady Mary, late wife to Sir Robert Vynor, now Lord Mayor of London, sickned on Munday last and died Jan. 1, 1674; a great loss to Sir Robert Vynor, she having during her life 2000*li.* p^r ann. and her only daughter by Mr. Hide having 4000*li.* p^r ann. (he being her former husbsnd). Her funerall on Tuesday Janua. 19, from Goldsmiths' Hall to St. Mary Wolnoth in Lombard Street.

3. This day was buried Luther Smith, a male child of

Thomas Smith, a millener wthout Bishopsgate, who died on Friday last, and was baptized the Sunday before (my sister Edney theire acquaintance), invited to the buriall; there born on Decem. 13 last.

8. Mis Moyer's old maide in Rope Makers' Alley, aged about 70 years, who had been servant to old Mis Moyer and son 50 years, was buried in Southwark; she was worth 400*li.* she had gott in her long service.

15. This day died the old Countess of Devonshire, at her house in Southampton Buildings in ye parish of St. Giles in the Fields.

Februa. 18. . . . . . . Philips, Judge of ye Sheriffs' Court in London, died.

19. Capt. Farre in Little Morefields buried.

1675.

March 26. Friday, old Mr. Richard Smith, my honoured friend, aged 85 years, dyed and was buried in Criplegate Church on ye 1st of April following; he was ye collector of the aforesaid Catalogue, and of many most excellent Books; he was a just man and of good report, and worthy of imitation.

AUGUSTIN NEWBOLD,

11 *Aprill,* 1675.

This Mr. Smith was secondary of y^e Poultry Compter about twenty years past.

A. N.

FINIS.

INDEX.

R

J. B. Nichols and Son, 25, Parliament Street.

9 781120 204288